"Your Own Devices"

"Your Own Devices"
a Life Manual

Denise Lammi and David Wojtowicz[66]

© Copyright 2006 Denise Lammi & David Wojtowicz.
All rights reserved. No part of this publication may be reproduced, stored in a retrieval system, or transmitted, in any form or by any means, electronic, mechanical, photocopying, recording, or otherwise, without the written prior permission of the author.

Note for Librarians: A cataloguing record for this book is available from Library and Archives Canada at www.collectionscanada.ca/amicus/index-e.html
ISBN 1-4120-9581-6

*Printed in Victoria, BC, Canada. Printed on paper with minimum 30% recycled fibre.
Trafford's print shop runs on "green energy" from solar, wind and other environmentally-friendly power sources.*

TRAFFORD
PUBLISHING

Offices in Canada, USA, Ireland and UK

Book sales for North America and international:
Trafford Publishing, 6E–2333 Government St.,
Victoria, BC V8T 4P4 CANADA
phone 250 383 6864 (toll-free 1 888 232 4444)
fax 250 383 6804; email to orders@trafford.com
Book sales in Europe:
Trafford Publishing (UK) Limited, 9 Park End Street, 2nd Floor
Oxford, UK OX1 1HH UNITED KINGDOM
phone 44 (0)1865 722 113 (local rate 0845 230 9601)
facsimile 44 (0)1865 722 868; info.uk@trafford.com
Order online at:
trafford.com/06-1336

10 9 8 7 6 5 4 3 2 1

You already possess all of the devices you need to live an optimum life; you need only put them to effective use.

Explore this manual to find out how.

CONTENTS

PREFACE   3

SECTION 1 - "HOW TO" for "YOU"   5
- Neuroscience   9
- Thoughts   12
- Filters   15
- Worry   17
- Instincts   21
- Integrity   24
- Rituals   27
- Health   31
- Stress   33
- Finding Answers   36
- Afterword   42

SECTION 2 – ENHANCE COMPATIBILITY AND PERFORMANCE WITH OTHER MAKES AND MODELS   43
- The Benefit of a Doubt   47
- Venting and Solving   50
- "Why Don't You? – Yes, But"   52
- Insecurity   55
- The Need to Blame   58
- Withdrawing   60
- Humour   61
- Mirroring   63
- Words   65
- Body Language   68
- Interrupting   71

- Cause and Effect — 74
- The Power Struggle — 76
- Afterword — 79

SECTION 3 - PROCEDURES AND BONUS FEATURES TO MAXIMIZE PERFORMANCE — 81
- Wonderment — 85
- Fun — 87
- Courage — 89
- You'll Never Please Everyone — 91
- The Meaning of Life — 94
- Happiness — 97
- Afterword — 100

SECTION – 4, TROUBLESHOOTING — 101
- Depression — 105
- Disappointments — 108
- Distortions — 112
- Poor Me — 114
- Negativity — 117
- Anger and Forgiveness — 122
- Grief, the Anger Stage — 124
- Nightmares — 126
- A Perfect Picture — 129
- Unsolvable Problems — 131
- Afterword — 134

FINAL WORDS — 135

APPENDIX I, FREQUENTLY ASKED QUESTIONS — 139

APPENDIX II, BIOS — 157

PREFACE

> *Man is buffeted by circumstances so long as he believes himself to be the creature of outside conditions, but when he realizes that he is a creative power, and that he may command the hidden soil and seeds of his being out of which circumstances grow; he then becomes the rightful master of himself.*
>
> James Allen [1]

A user guide or manual is a document intended to provide information about an application or system. "You" embody various applications and systems which are responsible for your feelings, thoughts, actions and state of being. The objective of this manual is to provide task oriented information about components of these applications and systems and the devices which operate them.

This manual is organized as follows:

Section 1, "How To" for "You":   This section identifies your tools and beneficial uses of them.

Section 2, Enhance Compatibility and Performance with Other Makes and Models: This section provides information about getting along with other people.

Section 3, Procedures and Bonus Features to Maximize Performance: This section describes advanced performance features included in your operating system.

Section 4, Troubleshooting: This section addresses possible problems that may be encountered and provides workable solutions.

Appendix I, Frequently Asked Questions: This appendix provides answers to questions that people often ask about life situations and provides a cross reference to the manual for additional information.

Appendix II, Bios: This appendix contains biographical information about the individuals quoted or referred to in the manual.

To get maximum results from this manual, it is recommended that you first read sections 1 to 4 and Appendix I of the manual. You may refer to Appendix II, as you read (when you want to know more about a particular individual quoted or mentioned). Afterwards, you should refer to components of the manual as a reference when you need direction in a particular area. The Table of Contents provides a list of the sections and topics which can be used to locate particular topics. In addition, you will find it useful to reread the entire manual from time to time as a refresher and, as you encounter new life experiences, to appreciate and understand the material in new ways.

> *Yesterday is gone. Tomorrow has not yet come. We have only today. Let us begin.*
>
> Mother Teresa [2]

SECTION - 1
"HOW TO" for "YOU"

"HOW TO" for "YOU"

"You" are a complicated and delicate instrument for which you never received an instruction manual. You are constantly manipulated by external and internal influences. Whether you know it or not, you possess all of the requisite tools to regulate and control these influences. This section will describe how to use these tools.

"You" possess both enabling and disabling attributes. Your enabling attributes are made up of your known (or perceived) abilities and talents and considerable unrealized abilities and talents that you possess. Some of these are unique to you as an individual but most are common to everyone. Your disabling attributes are those limiting perceptions and beliefs that you have that impose barriers. Some were taught to you; some you acquired through your own experiences.

The tools in this section were chosen with a view to:

1) discover or enhance your innate and learned abilities and
2) reveal or diffuse characteristics or beliefs that become your obstacles.

To what end? To help you live your life with more happiness, strength and courage.

"HOW TO" for "YOU"
Section Contents

- Neuroscience
- Thoughts
- Filters
- Worry
- Instincts
- Integrity
- Rituals
- Health
- Stress
- Finding Answers

Neuroscience

The tool: Neuroscience.

The task: Manipulate neuron connections.

Desired result: Strengthen desirable neuron connections and weaken undesirable neuron connections.

Change your thoughts and you change your world.

Norman Vincent Peale[3]

Neuroscience is the study of the brain and nervous system in relation to perception, memory, learning and behaviour. It is a very complicated area where ideas and scientific beliefs continue to evolve and there are many areas that lack clarity or proof and are subject to differences of opinion. However, everyone seems to agree that a thought is produced when brain neurons (nerve cells) produce a sort of electrical current (the neurons "fire") and form connections. Further, there is a tendency which is commonly described by the phrase *neurons that fire together, wire together*. This means that connections between neurons are strengthened when stimulated repeatedly. To put it another way; when neurons fire together, the connections between them strengthen and in the future those neurons will tend to fire together. Due to this behaviour of neurons, as the brain reacts to stimuli and makes decisions, it doesn't have to make a new decision with each stimulus because with repeated experience, it forms associations. (These associations might be considered to be good or bad.)

Further, neural connections are modified by what is learned through experience. As external stimuli arrive in the form of electrical currents from sensory cells they cause patterns of nerve impulses to be set up. These impulses can alter the strength of the connection between different neurons. While external stimuli influence the network of connections made, neurons are not merely connected or not connected. Rather, the nature of the synaptic connection between them determines whether one neuron firing has a strong or weak effect on the other (a strong or weak connection). A strong connection between two neurons means that it is more likely that if one of the neurons fires it will stimulate the other to fire. Accordingly, the connection between two neurons will strengthen if more often than not the two neurons fire together.

Due to the complexity of these neural networks, scientists don't know in detail how the individual firings of neurons and the connections to other neurons operate the brain. However, they do know that *neurons that fire together, wire together* and therefore repeating patterns occur when similar thoughts, feelings, and reactions are maintained over time.

Since neuron connections become stronger when they are practised, you can infer that if you practise happiness and positive thinking, you will have stronger neuron connections to support these emotions and they will come easier to invoke and sustain. Conversely, if you practise negative emotions; they will become more natural to you.

In other words, the more often you feel happy and positive, the more happy and positive you will become. This is certainly worth putting some effort towards because of the wonderful rewards. Think happy thoughts and think positive thoughts and they will become more and more natural to you!

We are, or become, those things which we repeatedly do. Therefore, excellence can become not just an event, but a habit.

Albert Einstein[4]

Thoughts

The tool:	Thoughts
The task:	Choose and encourage your own circumstances.
Desired result:	Positive circumstances.

> *As a man thinketh in his heart, so is he.*
>
> James Allen[1]

As a Man Thinketh was written by James Allen[1] over one hundred years ago (1904). He wrote that 'mind is the master weaver', which creates our inner character and outer circumstances. The logic is irrefutable. Happy thoughts make a happy person and miserable thoughts make a miserable person. To a person hampered by negativity, the world looks bleak. When negative and destructive thoughts are eliminated, the world becomes a better and friendlier place.

Thoughts have the power of attracting not only what you want, but also what you don't want. This is because thoughts, which receive your attention, whether they are good or bad, go into the subconscious as ideas. The subconscious looks for opportunities to manifest these ideas as events in the real world. Therefore, if you have positive thoughts, you are more likely to discover positive things. If you have fearful thoughts, you may find just what you were afraid of.

> *Every thought-seed sown or allowed to fall into the mind, and to take root there, produces its own, blossoming sooner or later into act, and bearing its own fruitage of opportunity and circumstance. Good thoughts bear good fruit, bad thoughts bad fruit.*
>
> James Allen[1]

The book is well written and contains many gems of wisdom.

The first gem comes from the introduction to the book when James Allen explains that the purpose of the book is to:

...stimulate men and women to the discovery and perception of the truth that "They themselves are makers of themselves" by virtue of the thoughts which they choose and encourage; that mind is the master-weaver, both of the inner garment of character and the outer garment of circumstance, and that, as they may have hitherto woven in ignorance and pain they may now weave in enlightenment and happiness.

The remaining gems are quotes from chapters in the book and are so well said that they stand on their own with no further explanation.

Circumstance does not make the man; it reveals him to himself.

Men are anxious to improve their circumstances, but are unwilling to improve themselves; they therefore remain bound.

Men imagine that thought can be kept secret, but it cannot. It rapidly crystallizes into habit, and habit solidifies into circumstance.

> *Whether you think that you can, or that you can't, you are usually right.*
>
> Henry Ford[5]

Filters

The tool: Identify your personal filters.

The task: Acknowledge your history without being controlled by it.

Desired result: View the world without looking through distorting filters.

> *Judgements prevent us from seeing the good that lies beyond appearances.*
>
> Dr. Wayne W. Dyer[6]

Dr. Phil McGraw[7] from the *Dr. Phil* show, on his website, wrote the following: "Identify the filters through which you view the world. Acknowledge your history without being controlled by it."

You know and experience this world through your own perceptions and you have the ability to choose how you perceive any event in your life. You exercise this power of choice in all circumstances, all of the time. You choose your reaction and evaluate each event. Dr. Phil refers to this as your own individual filters through which you view the world. These filters influence your interpretations, your responses, and in turn how others respond to you.

If you are aware of the factors that influence the way in which you see the world, you can compensate accordingly. Filters are often made up of erroneous beliefs and negative attitudes. You must be aware of this or else you will not seek, receive or process new information. When you view the world through a filter created by past events, past events then control and dictate your life.

If you look for the weaknesses in your belief system and attitudes, you can attempt to view the world without looking through distorting filters and you may then see more happiness and opportunities.

The eye sees only what the mind is prepared to comprehend.

Robertson Davies[8]

Worry

The tools:	Techniques to manage worry emotion.
The task:	Apply techniques at onset of worrisome thoughts.
Desired result:	Eliminate unproductive worry.

> *If we spend our time with regrets over yesterday, and worries over what might happen tomorrow, we have no today in which to live.*
>
> Author Unknown

Have you ever been unable to sleep because you were thinking about something that was bothering you? Have you ever left your house, drove to the airport, got on a plane and then wondered if you turned off the coffeepot? Something like it?

Worry can wear you down emotionally and physically. There are many ways that you can deal with worry. Some especially effective methods are summarized below.

The Wisdom of the Dalai Lama

The Dalai Lama[9] has been quoted as saying "If there is a solution to a problem, there is no need to worry. And if there is *no* solution, there is no need to worry."

His message is to focus on the solution and not the problem. However, when wrongs can't be righted or circumstances can't be controlled, one must accept the things they cannot change.

> *If there is a solution to a problem, there is no need to worry. And if there is no solution, there is no need to worry.*
>
> Dalai Lama[9]

The Logic of Statistics

Many people who have written or spoken about worry have told the statistics story. The earliest source that we could find of the story and most probable author was Thomas S. Kepler, a respected biblical scholar. He wrote about a woman who realized fears were ruining her life. She began to keep track of what was worrying her and she found:

40% of the things she worried about were about things that would never happen.

30% of the things she worried about were about things that had already happened, water under the bridge.

12% of the things she worried about were about others' opinions and when she thought about it she realized that criticisms are often made by those that are jealous or insecure and therefore unjust criticism is a disguised compliment.

10% of the things she worried about were needless health worries, which made her health worse as she worried.

8% of the things she worried about were "legitimate," since life has some real problems to meet.

If you consider the above as probable statistics, it would seem that only 8% of the things that you worry about are worth the worry. Next time you are worried about something, perform a check to see if the worry is in a category other then the 8% category and if it is, perhaps logic will help free you from the worry.

"Will This Matter a Year from Now?"

This idea comes from *Don't Sweat The Small Stuff* by Dr Richard Carlson[10]. You ask the question, "will this matter a year from now?". This provides a "check" on whether the circumstance that is causing worry is important. More often than not, the situation is not as important as you have made it out to be. Whether it is an argument, a mistake, a lost opportunity, a lost item, a rejection, or a sprained ankle - will it matter in a year from now? If not, the source of worry is probably just one more irrelevant detail in your life.

This approach does not solve problems, but it can put things into perspective. Dr. Carlson says he finds himself laughing at things that he used to take far too seriously and now, rather than using up energy feeling angry and overwhelmed, it can be used spending time with loved ones and creative thinking.

"What is the Worst That Can Possibly Happen?"

Dale Carnegie[11], in his book *How to Stop Worrying and Start Living*, credits this method to Willis Carrier (the man who invented the air conditioner). You start by asking the question, "What is the worst that can possibly happen?" To use an example, assume that in a business setting a mistake has been made which will impact a particular customer. In this example the answer to the question may be: the customer will get very angry, phone to yell and then take their business elsewhere. The next step is to get mentally prepared to accept this worst possible scenario, if necessary. Then, try to improve upon the worst. In this example you might call the customer before they call you, explain the situation, apologize and tell them how much you appreciate their business. Perhaps you could send them some small token of your appreciation (flowers or a cake?) or give them a special price or deal.

Instincts

The tool: Instinct.

The task: Listen to the voice inside.

Desired results: Identify danger. Identify opportunities.

> *Trust your hunches. They're usually based on facts filed away just below the conscious level.*
>
> Dr. Joyce Brothers[12]

You are very focused on the physical, logical, analytic world and yet sometimes you just get a "feeling" about something. You may dismiss it as, an illogical subconscious fear or desire, which is manifesting into conscious thought. (Your subconscious is the part of your mind which notices and remembers information without any deliberate action on your part; and influences your behaviour in ways unknown to you. Your conscious mind includes everything of which you are aware.) However, often you find that your "feelings" prove to be an accurate reading of a particular situation. Are these feelings premonitions? Likely, they are not. It is most likely that the "feelings" come from your subconscious, which has responded to some stimulus that has failed to impress upon your conscious mind.

These "feelings" can be good feelings or bad feelings. Often they are called "intuition" or a "gut feeling". To describe them, let's use the use the word "instinct" in the context of: *a powerful impulse that feels natural rather than reasoned.* However, while it may "feel" that the impulse is not "reasoned", it probably is and it is your conscious mind that has not recognized the reasons.

You should be very careful when you dismiss "bad feelings" because when it comes to your body or surroundings, your instincts may be warning you of danger. The world is not perfect. It is full of dangerous places, situations and people. Of course it is possible that your instincts are wrong. The important thing is to give instincts respect. That is not to say that your actions should revolve around good or bad feelings. Rather, when you have a feeling about something, it is a good idea to stop and take inventory of the situation. Reflect. Ask, "what is it that makes me feel uncomfortable or unsettled?" Such a pause may reveal clues or information that your conscious mind has previously overlooked.

Conversely, instincts may tell you of an opportunity. Sometimes something feels very right and later you look back and are glad that you pursued a particular path or later you look back and regret not listening to your instincts. That is not to say that you should pursue every whim with reckless abandon. Rather, when you have a good feeling about something and hesitate to act, stop and consider if your instincts are providing you with clues to information that you should consider.

You should "trust your instincts" to provide you with important insights.

You should be very careful when you dismiss "bad feelings" because when it comes to your body or surroundings, your instincts may be warning you of danger. The world is not perfect. It is full of dangerous places, situations and people.

> Conversely, instincts may tell you of an opportunity. Sometimes something feels very right and later you look back and are glad that you pursued a particular path or later you look back and regret not listening to your instincts.

Integrity

The tool:	Integrity.
The task:	Let honesty and compassion guide you.
Desired results:	Less anger, more control and happier relationships.

> *Better keep yourself clean and bright; you are the window through which you must see the world.*
>
> George Bernard Shaw[13]

Many have seen the movie Groundhog Day (where the character is forced to continuously re-live the worst day of his life until he learns to become a better person) but failed to recognize the important message of the movie.

Actor Bill Murray plays Phil, an unpleasant weather forecaster who must spend the night in Punxsutawney, Pennsylvania, in order to do a broadcast the next morning about the annual event of the groundhog. He wakes, does his story and is later very annoyed to discover that he is trapped in Punxsutawney for a second night because of a snowstorm. But when he wakes up the next morning, it is the morning of the day before all over again. Everything that happened to him the previous day, all happens again. And again, the snowstorm forces him to spend the night in Punxsutawney.

He is trapped in a time loop and every morning he wakes up on Groundhog Day. He is the only one that remembers what happened in previous versions of the same day. If he does nothing different, events repeat themselves as they were on the original day. But when he changes how he behaves, people respond accordingly.

At first Phil undergoes bewilderment, then despair. He risks his life, binges on food ... no matter what he does; he wakes up as if nothing had happened. Groundhog days pass one after another and then Phil finds a purpose in life ... he sets out to learn everything that there is to know about his producer, Rita, (played by Andie MacDowell). He calculates that if he can trick her into believing that he is her ideal man, he can seduce her. His deceitful behaviour is not rewarded.

He goes back to despair and spends his days killing himself. He kidnaps the groundhog and drives over a cliff, he takes a plugged-in toaster into the bath ... no matter what he does, he always wakes up intact in the morning. He finally figures out a better way to deal with the time loop. He begins to live his life each day in the time allotted. Instead of allowing circumstances to impose on him, he takes control of circumstances.

He takes piano lessons. He learns ice sculpting. When he discovers that an old man dies on his day, he can't accept the man's death. The next day, he is kind to the old man. He feeds him well and tries to keep him alive. The old man still dies.

When Phil realizes he can't fight death, he transfers his compassion for the old man to the living.

He begins to use his knowledge of what happens on the day to help people. He knows that a child will always fall from a tree at a certain time so he is always there to catch the child. He knows that a man will choke on his meal and so he is always at a nearby table to save him.

Phil is transformed. Rita falls in love with the good person he has become. It is then that when he wakes up, it is the next morning, February 3, the day after Groundhog Day.

This movie serves to illustrate how letting go of anger and resentment and choosing to live life with authenticity and compassion can result in gaining control of your life and happiness.

> But when he changes how he behaves, people respond accordingly.

> *It's not enough to have lived. We should be determined to live for something. May I suggest that it be creating joy for others, sharing what we have for the betterment of personkind, bringing hope to the lost and love to the lonely.*
>
> Leo Buscaglia[14]

Rituals

The tool:	Rituals.
The task:	Add substance and meaning to actions and events at both the individual and social level.
Desired result:	Enrich your life and have a sense of belonging to community.

> *I don't believe people are looking for the meaning of life as much as they are looking for the experience of being alive.*
>
> Joseph Campbell[15]

Rituals are procedures performed which "act out" thoughts or beliefs. These thoughts or beliefs may also be referred to as ideas or myths. These ideas and the resultant rituals add meaning to behaviours or events. Rituals can convert an otherwise ordinary or practical event into something that has a meaning that goes beyond what separate actions add up to. In other words, there is a synergy because the actions producing a ritual stimulate emotions and add colour to transform that which might otherwise be bland events into meaningful events. Rituals are the basis of traditions. Rituals and tradition provide an opportunity to make important events special and memorable. Due to certain similarities, people will generally have similar responses to ritualized events and their symbols.

Why do people perform a particular ritual? What are the ideas or myths that created the occasion to perform the ritual? Do you need to know? If you know, what do you do with the knowledge? Do you continue to celebrate the event by maintaining the myth and the ritual that accompanies it? Or, do you discard the myth and related ritual as nonsense that has no relevance to your life? Or, since you have a choice, should you keep certain rituals? - The general consensus is that you would be wise to keep and revere that which has meaning and purpose for your life and/or gives you a sense of belonging to society. Myth, ritual and tradition need to be considered for what they were intended to represent and should be encouraged where the objective is to bring desirable meaning and purpose to life.

Rituals can provide substance and meaning to life at both the individual and social level. Ritual and its symbols therefore act as a means by which values and structures of society can continue through the ages. Rituals can also create new values and structures. These values, whether traditional or new, can be transmitted to individuals.

Myth and ritual can satisfy individual needs in everyday life. Whether you are conscious of it or not, you have certain personal myths and shared myths concerning your own identity and you perform certain rituals to enhance these myths. (E.g. carrying a sentimental item, wearing a certain clothing item for luck, performing certain routines in a particular order, making your bed every morning, closing each email with the same goodbye.) Daily living is filled with mini ceremonies (ritualistic acts), that bring you out of the ordinary and connect you to yourself and the world. By expressing these otherwise unexceptional actions with purposefulness awareness and affection, your life gains meaning.

Life brings changes. All over the world, past and present, cultures or societies have rituals (ceremonies) signifying an event in a person's life indicative of a transition from one stage to another. These are often referred to as "rites of passage". Rites of passage provide purpose and function at both the individual and the group level by revealing the change in a positive light. Also, it is natural to experience stresses in connection with undergoing change and rites of passage assist people in coping with the stress and provide meaning for the change. Examples of rites of passage include graduation ceremonies, bar mitzvahs, weddings, retirement parties and funerals. Such events lose their real meaning and impact when you just go through the motions and do not appreciate the significance of the transition. Incomplete rituals and therefore incomplete transitions do not facilitate the acceptance of the change.

> *Rituals help us celebrate, and at the other end of the spectrum they help us to connect deeply with people in times of sorrow. The repetition that ritual always involves sets the present moment in a larger context and infuses it with wider meaning.*
>
> Huston Smith[16]

Rituals are often dismissed as primitive, unnecessary or religious. However, since myth and ritual can be valuable instruments to enrich your own life and give you a sense of belonging to community, before you dismiss or discard a ritual, you should stop to consider the meaning and effect of the ritual. Disowning rituals operates to disassociate you from yourself and from other people.

> Disowning rituals operates to disassociate you from yourself and from other people.

Health

The tool:	Your body.
The task:	Attention to diet and exercise.
Desired result:	Maintain body strength and mobility.

> *Lack of activity destroys the good condition of every human being, while movement and methodical physical exercise save it and preserve it.*
>
> Plato[17]

You undergo bodily changes that cause you to go through the stages of the human life cycle (infancy, childhood, adolescence, young adulthood, maturity and old age). The length of time that you spend in each of these stages, especially those after adolescence, is not fixed. It is dependent on factors that include genes, culture, environment and attitude.

Due to your human condition and the resultant stages of life; physical changes that will eventually result in physical impairment are unavoidable. However, you do have significant control over the commencement and rate of change. Attention to diet and exercise will prolong vitality whereas a lack of attention to diet and exercise will accelerate physical decline.

Do not lose your mobility and freedom prematurely by your own hand. Obesity, high blood pressure and atrophy are just a few ways in which you can do so; if you are careless.

You should keep your good health as long as you can.

Stress

The tool:	Stress reduction.
The task:	Reduce or eliminate destructive stress.
Desired result:	Healthier mind and body.

> *If you ask what is the single most important key to longevity, I would have to say it is avoiding worry, stress and tension. And if you didn't ask me, I'd still have to say it.*
>
> George Burns[18]

Stress is destructive to health and relationships. Stress is experienced when a person feels demands and expectations that exceed perceived available resources. Resources may relate to time, money, skill, tools, etc. The perception of the imbalance between the demands and resources and potential future adverse consequences for failing to meet the demand or expectation does not have to be correct in order for the situation to cause stress. That is, false understandings or beliefs can cause significant stress. Therefore any event or thought that causes a person to perceive a threatening demand is a potential source of stress.

It is true that on this planet there are situations that need to be reacted to and in the absence of stress, our species would never have survived. Accordingly, a positive aspect of stress is that it alerts you to a threat and provides you with increased levels of energy and motivation to help in coping with the threat. However mishandled stress or too much stress causes strain and can be devastating for you.

The negative effects of stress are numerous and perhaps we don't even know them all. However, they include fatigue, irritability, anger, difficulty concentrating, a lower immune system, a variety of serious physical health problems, insomnia, depression, anxiety, loss of personal relationships, over eating and drug and alcohol abuse.

There is no one way to deal with stress. Stress may be reduced, eliminated or managed by addressing one or more of the underlying components of stress. For example you might reduce demands by planning ahead, increasing available resources, just saying "no", finding ways to increase efficiency. Or, you might reduce the stress emotions by taking a break from the stressful situation, relaxing, exercising, getting a massage, taking a vacation. Or, you might eliminate or mitigate the impact of the consequences of failing to meet the demand by preparing for the consequences (e.g. having a savings account or buying insurance), changing your priorities (so what if the car doesn't get washed?), accepting what can't be changed, putting energy towards improving the situation.

You need to have the correct perspective concerning the demands you face. You need to be aware of your capabilities, resources, and the real consequences of failing to meet a demand. You need to see things accurately without distortions. Believing something is terrible when it is only just unpleasant can cause unnecessary stress.

There is scientific evidence that suggests that the experience of stress in the past magnifies how you react to stress in the future because stress actually alters your body and your brain. You can become sensitive to stress and then even the smallest stressor can invoke reactions in your brain and body that cause your brain to treat a small incident as a life threatening event. Because some stress is requisite for humans, your body is designed to provide an appropriate reaction to stress depending on the degree of the threat. However, when you become sensitive to stress due to earlier stress experiences, your body's response that is designed for life threatening events is activated by ordinary trials and tribulations of life such that you respond inappropriately (in other words, overreact). This sensitivity to stress may begin during childhood. It is likely that the impact is greater when it is initiated during childhood.

It is of extreme importance that you become aware of your body so that you can sense when it is getting stressed and either reduce the stressors (i.e. demands perceived to exceed resources and perceived negative consequences) or take time for meditation, yoga, exercise, gardening, reading, writing, listening to music, going for a walk. Also, the knowledge about being sensitive to stress due to past stress experiences (i.e. the life-death reaction to inconsequential matters) is helpful, if it applies to you, because you can use logic and rational thoughts to understand why you're reacting as you are and to correct this behaviour if you feel yourself overreacting to stressors.

You are vulnerable to stress and will experience stress; but you do not have to be its victim. You have the ability to control stress and what you permit it to do to you.

Finding Answers

The tools:	1. Incubation.
	2. Sleep on it.
	3. Look anywhere.
The task:	Find answers.
Desired result:	Effectively solve problems or access information.

No problem can stand the assault of sustained thinking.

Voltaire[19]

Much of life involves questions and uncertainty. Proficiency in finding answers, resolving issues or solving problems enables you to reduce or eliminate many negative influences in your life such as stress and worry. It also enables you to have more control over your life.

How you find, resolve or solve will depend on the nature of the matter, your talents and resources available to you. The tools described below may be of assistance.

1. Incubation

Graham Wallas[20], in his book *The Art of Thought (1926)*, described problem solving as containing four distinct stages: Preparation,

Incubation, Illumination and Verification. Since his book; others have refined, added and adapted these ideas to current research. Understanding the Incubation stage in particular is extremely useful. A summary of the four stages described by Wallas and where incubation fits will explain how incubation works.

1) Preparation
The problem is defined, information is collected and possible approaches are considered. The problem solver is occupied with thinking about the issue.

2) Incubation
Attention is turned away from the problem and towards other subjects. The problem solver, on the conscious level, mentally lets go of the problem and focuses attention on other subjects. Sometimes this takes a short while like seconds or minutes. Other times, it takes days or weeks.

3) Illumination
The light bulb comes on. The solution is suddenly apparent.

4) Verification
The solution is checked to confirm that it works.

During the incubation stage, the subconscious continues to work on the problem even though the conscious mind has moved on to other matters. In other words, problem solving performance is improved after temporarily putting a problem aside. Just think; you don't have to keep directly applying yourself to solve a problem - you can delegate to your subconscious and go out to play! This is an excellent design feature of the human brain.

> During the Incubation stage, the subconscious continues to work on the problem even though the conscious mind has moved on to other matters.

2. Sleep on It

> *Take thy thoughts to bed with thee, for the morning is wiser than the evening.*
>
> Russian Proverb

You can solve problems while you sleep. Your brain is especially creative while you are sleeping. This includes times when you are falling asleep or waking up and deeper dream states. Possible explanations for this include:

1. Your brain is not dealing with external influences such as sights and sounds and can direct more resources to creativity.

2. Your conscious and subconscious are both fluid during the sleep state and the synergy of the two creates a greater data base for your mind to draw from. Formal knowledge, personal knowledge, observations, experiences, learned skills, ideals, values and everything else in your head are all present and available.

3. Your subconscious observes and remembers details

unknown to your conscious, which you can not retrieve at will.

4. There is transference of information between your conscious and subconscious during relaxed states.

5. It was previously described how solutions surface during the Illumination stage of problem solving. This Illumination stage operates best during relaxed periods. What could be a more relaxed period than sleep?

6. Your subconscious does not lack confidence whereas your conscious may. Your subconscious doesn't think that you may not be good enough or smart enough.

Many people have used dreams to solve problems or recall lost memories. Through dreams; mathematical problems have been solved, golf swings have been perfected, winning legal arguments have been conceived, items have been invented, physics models have been conceptualized, chemical properties have been realized, elements have been classified, lost valuables have been found – the list goes on and on.

If discoveries, lost memories or inspirations come to you when you are sleeping; to get the most benefit from the dream knowledge you need to recall the dream. If you have difficulty recalling dreams, you may find that, like anything; if you practice you will become more proficient in dream recall. Some people keep paper and pen beside their bed to write down the dream idea because they don't trust themselves to remember the idea.

What if you have a brilliant idea while dreaming and you aren't able to recall it? It is possible that mere process of the brain activity directed towards the brilliant idea is enough for your conscious to access the information at a later time when stimulated. But rather than take this chance, it is advisable to practise dream recall or use paper and pen.

3. Look Anywhere

> *The answers you get from literature depend on the questions you pose.*
>
> Margaret Atwood[21]

When you have a decision to make and you seek guidance for your answer, where do you look? Perhaps you turn to spiritual resources such as the Bible, the Koran or the teachings of Buddha. Perhaps you ask a friend or mentor, see a therapist, read a book, climb a mountain, go camping in the woods and so on.

If you sincerely look for such an answer, you will find it no matter where you look. That is because the answer is already within you and you are really just looking for an outlet through which to discover that which you already know. This means that the answer may be found almost anywhere. It may well be that if you open any book on any page; you will find clues to the answer that you seek.

The fact that an answer may be found almost anywhere explains why people often see "a sign" to guide them. You needn't be religious to believe in the veracity of signs. If you ponder and consider a situation and sincerely want an answer, you will find it. It may come to you in a dream, a movie, a book, a lecture, a rock formation, a comment made by a stranger and so on.

> ... the answer is already within you and you are really just looking for an outlet through which to discover that which you already know.

Afterword

The tools described in this section are already within you. You just have to apply them. Information regarding their applications is not new. Rather it is some of the best of what past and present thinkers have left as a legacy to us. The tools are not difficult to use. You just have to remember to use them. Doing so will help you enjoy life more.

> *The greatest discovery of my generation is that a human being can alter his life by altering his attitude of mind.*
>
> William James[22]

SECTION - 2

ENHANCE COMPATIBILITY AND PERFORMANCE WITH OTHER MAKES AND MODELS

ENHANCE COMPATIBILITY AND PERFORMANCE WITH OTHER MAKES AND MODELS

In the beginning of Section 1 it was pointed out that you are a complicated and delicate instrument. It should be no surprise to you; that other people are also complicated and delicate. It probably seems to you; that they are especially so.

Likely, the greatest external influence manipulating you is other people. They have their own thoughts, perceptions, expectations, strengths and weaknesses.

Much of your success in many aspects of life depends on how effectively you deal with other people. This section identifies common compatibility issues and provides practical instructions to improve interactions.

...OTHER MAKES AND MODELS
Section Contents

- The Benefit of a Doubt
- Venting and Solving
- "Why Don't You? – Yes, But"
- Insecurity
- The Need to Blame
- Withdrawing
- Humour
- Mirroring
- Words
- Body Language
- Interrupting
- Cause and Effect
- The Power Struggle

The Benefit of a Doubt

Compatibility issue: Personalizing another person's behaviour creates a chain reaction of system breakdowns.

Resolution: Give others the benefit of a doubt. Do not assume that you are the source or target for another's anger.

> *Any fool can criticize, condemn, and complain but it takes character and self control to be understanding and forgiving.*
>
> Dale Carnegie[11]

Remember to give other people the benefit of a doubt. Unfortunately, it is easy to forget. The result is that you may view someone's behaviour as a personal attack and get angry.

Imagine that last night you were woken at 2 AM by the loud music of your neighbour who had just come home from the bar and was entertaining friends. You fume and fret. You can't block out the noise and go back to sleep. Maybe you call the building manager, maybe you knock at your neighbour's door. Maybe you call the police. It doesn't matter. You're upset and when you go to work in the morning you're tired and CRANKY.

You attend the morning meeting to discuss the results of the last quarter. You imply that your staff let you down. That wasn't your planned approach but that's how it comes out. Martha, one of the attendees is very disappointed. She had worked very hard in the past few months and had hoped that her efforts would be recognized.

Martha goes back to her office. Her secretary, Michelle, asks if it would be OK to work an extra hour each day for the rest of this week so that she can take Friday afternoon off. Martha says "We have a business to run. I need you here to type the reports that his holiness has requested. I'm sorry that the company is interfering with your personal life!"

Later that morning, Michelle's husband Gerry calls to ask if she got Friday afternoon off. Michelle says "No and I know that you make more money than me and think my job isn't very important. Well it is important and I have commitments and responsibilities you know."

Poor Gerry. He goes to his doctor's appointment. After 45 minutes he's still in the waiting room. He goes up to the woman at the reception desk and asks how much longer. When he's told she doesn't know, he's livid. He takes his anger out on her. Doris, the receptionist, is particularly sensitive because she's been dealing with upset patients all day.

When Doris' sister Betty calls to ask if Doris can baby-sit that night, Doris accuses Betty of taking advantage of her.

And so on.

Each of the characters in this story reacted to the other person's anger by taking it personally. In doing so, they created a chain reaction. Any one of these characters could have stopped the chain reaction if they had given the other person the benefit of a doubt and not assumed the anger was about them. In the story we used examples of people behaving badly in a particular situation. In life, it's often not just one situation. Rather, the person may repeatedly exhibit bad behaviour. It's important to remember that there may be trials and tribulations in a person's life (past or present) of which you have no idea. Rather than assume the worst about a person's character, it's better to give them the benefit of a doubt. There is always more to the situation – you only see a part of the other person's reality.

That is why you should always try to remember that criticism, anger or venom that you receive from another person is often not about you. It is better to understand this than to take the communication personally and ruin your day as well as the day of others that you come into contact with.

Criticism, anger or venom that you receive from another person is often not about you. Give people the benefit of a doubt.

Venting and Solving

Compatibility issue: Venting misinterpreted as a request for advice.

Resolution: Listening.

> *When we ask for advice, we are usually looking for an accomplice.*
>
> Charles Varlet Marquis de La Grange[23]

Sometimes people just want to complain and aren't looking for solutions. To these people, sharing problems with others is a sign of friendship and trust. They are not looking for advice. They just want to be listened to. Some people are natural born problem solvers or feel a responsibility to respond when they perceive that they are being asked for help and therefore find themselves giving advice which is not well received. They may even feel responsible for causing the problems or responsible to solve the problems. They offer explanations or solutions instead of just listening.

Often when a person vents about a problem, they want someone to agree with them or at least acknowledge that they understand the frustration. They feel that if they wanted advice, they would ask for it. Conversely, when on the receiving end of someone's venting session one may believe that they have some very good solutions or suggestions. Accordingly, this is an area where misunderstandings can happen very easily. Unsolicited advice may offend the person it is given to, as it may seem critical or judgmental. Ignored or unwanted advice may offend the person giving it, as it may seem unappreciated or unvalued.

You should be able to be a good listener without offering solutions. As a good listener, you should focus on trying to understand what the person is going through. Of course sometimes a person really does want advice or there is something that you know that could make things much better. You have to rely on your listening and communicating skills to figure out when to just listen and when to offer advice. If the person is very angry or excited when speaking, they may just want to vent whereas if the person is calm or analytical when speaking, they may be looking for advice or be in a position to accept it in the spirit it is given. If uncertain whether it is advice that is being solicited or just good listening, you might consider asking the person whether they've reached the stage with their problem such that they are ready to start considering solutions.

It is also important to recognize that sometimes there really is no problem. The venting or complaining person just wants to unload some stresses or frustrations. For example, if someone wants to complain about stresses at work, they may not find it very helpful if you offer the advice "then you should quit and find a new job".

> As a good listener, you should focus on trying to understand what the person is going through.

"Why Don't You? – Yes, But"

Compatibility issue: Meaningful communication breaks down when interaction becomes tantamount to a game.

Resolution: Recognize the game and choose not to play.

The word 'but' negates everything that precedes it.

…the reason why communication experts suggest that you avoid the use of the word 'but'.

Sometimes the venting/solving interaction with other people takes on the form of a game. For example, many people play the "Why don't you? – Yes, but" game. You may have unwittingly played both sides of this game without even noticing that the particular interaction is like a game. The following example dialogue of the game comes from the book *Games People Play* by Dr. Eric Berne[24].

White: "My husband always insists on doing our own repairs, and he never builds anything right."

Black: "Why doesn't he take a course in carpentry?"

White: "Yes, but he doesn't have time."

Blue: "Why don't you buy him some good tools?"

White: "Yes, but he doesn't know how to use them."

Red: "Why don't you have your building done by a carpenter?"

White: "Yes, but that would cost too much."

Brown: "Why don't you just accept what he does the way he does it?"

White: "Yes, but the whole thing might fall down."

According to Dr. Berne, any number of people can play this game. He says, "a good player can stand off the others indefinitely until they all give up, whereupon White wins." He also says that since the solutions are almost always rejected the game must serve some ulterior purpose and is not being played in order for White to garner information or solutions, as she would have you think. Rather, it is played to reassure and gratify the "child" aspect of White's character. White presents herself as a child incapable of dealing with the situation and the others then take on the role of parents anxious to give advice. (The child does not want to be dominated and the parent tries to dominate the child, but fails.) He says the game is very popular because at the social level, all players behave as adults and at the psychological level, the parent child combination is complementary. Usually, White is as intelligent as the other players and it is unlikely that the other players will suggest anything she has not already thought of. If someone comes up with an original suggestion and White is playing fair, the adult side of her should concede. However, players such as White seldom play fair because (in the words of Dr. Berne) "The purpose of the game is not to get suggestions, but to reject them." White wins when no more solutions are forthcoming, the parents have failed.

If one doesn't want to play this game in a social setting, the game may be avoided. To go back the dialogue at the beginning, what if it went like this?

White: "My husband always insists on doing our own repairs, and he never builds anything right."

Black: "That is a difficult problem. What are you going to do about it?"

In this example, the game never gets off the ground. Dr. Berne says that in a social setting the game is generally harmless and there is no reason not to participate. However, when you think about your own experiences, (before learning about the game), you may have felt frustrated in the role of White, the child, because the other players would continue on with solutions that you had already thought of or that were impractical. Now that you know, you can terminate the game by just saying "thank you for the suggestion" instead of feeding those playing the part of the wise and helpful parents. You may also have felt frustrated in the role of the wise and helpful parent because you felt that White had dismissed your suggestions too easily. Now you can see that this particular frustration was because, even at the time, you realized that White wasn't really playing fairly.

> ...the game is very popular because at the social level, all players behave as adults and at the psychological level, the parent child combination is complementary.

Insecurity

Compatibility issues: Feelings of insecurity may cause various compensatory behaviours such as being judgemental, arrogant or shy.

Resolution: You should tackle your own insecure feelings at their source (see Section 1 for tools) and recognize that certain behaviours from others may be due to their insecure feelings.

> *Our greatest pretenses are built up not to hide the evil and the ugly in us, but our emptiness. The hardest thing to hide is something that is not there.*
>
> Eric Hoffer[25]

Why does a person gossip, judge, disparage or otherwise speak negatively about someone else? Why do they discriminate against others because of race, religion, or body type? The answer is low self-esteem. Those with low self-esteem routinely diminish people in other groups or stations to distance themselves and gain standing. That way, everyone outside of their faction is in some way inferior to them. This creates, for them, the self-esteem which they seek, albeit artificial. They feel superior by being one of the "good guys" or not being one of the "bad guys". Therefore, those who constantly criticize others are trying to boost their relative standing so that they can feel better about themselves. It is easy to see how those that unnecessarily criticize, ridicule or otherwise mistreat others are displacing their own insecurities (that manifests as anxieties and fears) onto others - whether they do so consciously or unconsciously. The difficult thing to see is how you are guilty of this behaviour. You will experience insecurity from time to time and seek validation and reinforcement. The question is: will you try to make yourself look and/or feel better at the expense of someone else? The next time that you disparage someone, think about it.

People are insecure for various reasons and overcompensate for their insecure feelings in various ways. Another method that a person may overcompensate is to conduct himself or herself as superior. They may try to appear more intelligent or more worldly. They may try to appear to have more stamina. They may appear more serious and not laugh or relate to others. Unfortunately, others perceive such behaviour as arrogant or "stand-offish" when actually the behaviour is a reaction to insecure feelings. These "stand-offish" people are feeling inferior, afraid and alone. There are many reasons why this may be the case. The important thing to remember is that these people have feelings too. Like all of us, they want love, attention and a sense of belonging. The more that these needs are not met, the stiffer they appear because inside they are hurt and feel the need to convert their pain into hardness to survive. The stiff behaviour discourages others from getting close all the more. It's a vicious circle - the more they hurt, the more they push others away; and the more they push others away, the more they hurt.

Similarly, insecurity may cause shyness and social withdrawal and this may be interpreted as arrogance.

People with high self-esteem who are secure in their beliefs and own self worth feel no need to disparage others or distance themselves from others in order to validate themselves.

> People with high self-esteem who are secure in their beliefs and own self worth feel no need to disparage others or distance themselves from others in order to validate themselves.

The Need to Blame

Compatibility Issue: The need to place blame on others.

Resolution: Deal with the real problem that underlies the need to blame.

A man may fall many times, but he won't be a failure until he says that someone pushed him.

Elmer G. Letterman[26]

There is a tendency in many people to find someone to blame when bad things happen. When an unfortunate incident occurs and no one has acted carelessly or maliciously, there is no point to assigning blame. Misdirected feelings of insecurity, anger or embarrassment are often the cause of one person blaming another.

While blaming someone for your misfortunes provides an outlet to vent your anger or frustration, the relief is temporary at best. The destructive nature of blaming someone else can have far reaching ramifications. Blaming someone doesn't deal with the real problem at hand and it wastes energy that can be used to rectify the problem or prevent a similar occurrence in the future. Blaming causes hard feelings, compromises relationships and creates unnecessary conflicts. It feeds insecurity and guilt feelings in others. It can have a severe impact on children when experienced during their development because it causes them to take on unnecessary responsibility for the well being of others and feel guilt for bad events that are outside of their control.

You should see blaming for the mean-spirited, aggressive, bully-like behaviour that it is. The feelings that caused the blaming should be dealt with and not just vented by blaming.

You should see blaming for the mean-spirited, aggressive, bully-like behaviour that it is.

Withdrawing

Compatibility issue: Withdrawal of others.

Resolution: Patience.

Some people deal with frustrations or stress by withdrawing. They may not want to talk. It could be that they don't want to burden others with their problems. They feel that they need to solve problems alone or they need to spend some time thinking before they reach out to someone else. They can become distant and unresponsive to everything and everyone around them. Family and friends may resent this but they need to understand the situation. Often if the person is allowed to withdraw as needed, they will initiate communication after they have had time to process the issue. As a good friend, family member or work colleague; you should be patient for this to happen and be ready and available to listen or offer suggestions when approached.

It is not to say that the person that has withdrawn should be ignored. You want them to know that they have your understanding and support. You want to ensure that openings or opportunities exist for the person to talk if they are so inclined. You want to convey the message that you care and want to help but that you will give them their space.

He who does not understand your silence will probably not understand your words.

Elbert Hubbard[27]

Humour

Compatibility Issue:	Bad humour may invoke hurt feelings.
Resolution:	Recognize the different reasons humour is invoked. Avoid communicating with humour as an act of aggression and treat the receipt of such aggression as any other act of aggression.

Bad humour is an evasion of reality; good humour is an acceptance of it.

Malcolm Muggeridge[28]

Humour is often used to communicate. Sometimes you may feel proud, loved or relieved by a humorous remark. Other times, you may feel hurt, offended or confused by being the object of a humorous remark. Similarly, your humour remarks may cause the same feelings in others.

The reason that humour can invoke different feelings is that humour is invoked for different reasons.

Some of the reasons humour is invoked include:

1. A defense - a coping mechanism to manage or deflect that which is beyond one's control. For example, humour can be used to transform a bad situation into

something that is easier to cope with. Generally speaking, this can be a good thing provided that a person does not hide behind humour in a state of denial.

2. An attack - an aggressive act. For example, bad humour can be used to insult or put someone down. Aggression is usually indicative of underlying problems such as anger, pain, frustration or fear. Just because a mean-spirited remark is hidden behind the veil of humour, it doesn't make it any less mean-spirited. Bullies use humour to ridicule.

3. To connect - a way to connect or endear others. For example, humour can refer to a commonly shared experience or concern and promote bonding. Sometimes there is a fine line between jovial bantering and offensive comments. It is important to be attentive to the other person's reaction to the humour.

Humour is a complicated subject because 1) that which makes things funny is complicated and 2) the reasons that people communicate humourously is complicated. The important thing to remember is that humour is a form of communication and the veil of humour should not hide either good or bad intentions. In particular, when it comes to aggressive, bully-like remarks, you must recognize them for what they are and treat them as any other offensive act regardless of whether you are on the giving end or the receiving end.

Mirroring

Compatibility issue: Dislike for certain characteristics of others.

Resolution: Determine if you also possess the offensive characteristics.

> ...none of us can stand other people having the same faults as ourselves.
>
> Oscar Wilde[29]

Are there people that really irritate you and "push your buttons"? Do they seem to bother you more than they bother others? If so, it may be that these troublesome people are seen as such by you because you see in them, what you don't like about yourself, and have not consciously recognized. This is called "mirroring".

It is easy to understand what mirroring is but it is difficult to remember to apply it. If you remember to consider and interpret the valuable information that can be gained, you can find an opportunity to better understand yourself and the reason that the other person irritates you. Once you address the problem, which has been mirrored, you often find that the mirroring person is no longer offensive to you.

Therefore, when you recognize negative characteristics in others, you should consider the possibility that you also possess the same negative characteristics. You may find it reassuring to know that the degree or magnitude of the offensive behaviour is not necessarily mirrored. That is, often the negative characteristics of the other person are exaggerated compared to those of the person that recognized the characteristics.

Examples of behaviour that you may find offensive in others (and may also be harbouring within you) are arrogant, demanding, contrary, confrontational, aggressive, weak, interrupting…behaviour.

Recognizing your own character deficiencies gives you an opportunity to improve yourself. However, every character flaw that you identify in others is not necessarily a character flaw of your own. The important part about thinking in terms of mirroring is to become more attentive to what you don't like in others, and consider if there is a possibility that you may share that particular flaw or deficiency or in positive terms – if it is an area for personal improvement.

> Once one addresses the problem, which has been mirrored, they often find that the mirroring person is no longer offensive to them.

> *When looking for faults use a mirror, not a telescope.*
>
> Author Unknown

Words

Compatibility Issue: Words communicate intended or unintended meanings.

Resolution: Consider the meaning of words to the listener.

> *A word is not a crystal, transparent and unchanged; it is the skin of a living thought and may vary greatly in color and content according to the circumstances and the time in which it is used.*
>
> Oliver Wendell Holmes, Jr.[30]

You can use words to diffuse an angry person, make someone feel proud, give them a confidence boost or make them feel happy and giddy. You can also use words in the opposite way. You can rile a person to anger, make someone feel blamed or accused, make them feel inadequate or cause them anxiety and unhappiness. Therefore, it is important to remember the power and impact of words when choosing them.

Naturally, choosing appropriate words is all just common sense. However, you may sometimes forget just how much impact you can have on others. For example, when someone is angry at a situation, the person is likely to get angrier if his or her concerns are not validated. Choosing words such as "I can understand that this is frustrating", "I can appreciate what you're saying" or "I've felt that way too" can help calm someone down.

When asking questions, you should avoid words that frame the question in an accusatory, judgmental manner. For example if you ask, "Why didn't you...?", the person will likely react by going into a defensive mode. This is neither productive nor pleasant. Therefore, questions that begin with "why" should be used cautiously because they have the potential to make people defensive or feel like they have to explain themselves. It is better to begin the question with "what".

When someone is upset, you should choose words that don't suggest they are to blame. Upset people are not in a position to acknowledge their faults. Don't say things like "you should have" or "you didn't". These come off as accusatory and will only put someone on the defensive.

Remember how you felt when someone complimented you on something? Isn't it wonderful? Not just a compliment about new shoes or a new hairdo (which are also very nice to receive); rather, when someone said something to you like "you did an excellent job" or "thank you, I couldn't have done it without you". Sometimes people don't say these things because they think the other person already knows. If you can make someone feel happy or confident or proud by stating the obvious, why not do it? Don't be miserly with your compliments or words of encouragement, they cost you nothing but have great value to those who receive them.

> Don't be miserly with your compliments or words of encouragement, they cost you nothing but have great value to those who receive them.

YOUR OWN DEVICES

> *They may forget what you said, but they will never forget how you made them feel.*
>
> Carl W. Buechner[31]

Body Language

Compatibility issue: Words are the most common way to communicate meanings but are often deficient or don't really represent a person's thoughts.

Resolution: Be attentive to all forms of communication from others.

The human body is the best picture of the human soul.

Ludwig Wittgenstein[32]

"Body language" is gestures, facial expressions, posture and everything that isn't spoken. The following are common examples of what a particular body movement might reveal. However, for different people in different circumstances, it may mean something different entirely.

 Arms crossed on chest - Defensiveness
 Leaning forward in chair - Attentiveness
 Tilted head - Interest
 Brisk, erect walk - Confidence
 Biting nails or cuticles - Nervousness, insecurity
 Hands in pockets, shoulders hunched - Dejection
 Standing, hands on hips - Readiness, aggression

People use body language to express themselves (intentionally or unintentionally) and to gain meaning from others. An awareness of body language is useful. It can be particularly useful in sales, reading an audience, job interviews, meetings, socializing and relationships. For example, consider one particular area of body language - the "closed body posture" (e.g. arms crossed). "Closed body posture" is easy to watch for and reversing it can have great rewards. Closed-off posture usually reveals a close-minded attitude (e.g. defensive, suspicious). Open posture usually reveals an open or willing attitude. When people are in the closed state they are not receptive. When the objective is to communicate information or achieve a particular result (such as making a sale or convincing your partner that remodelling the kitchen is a good idea), it is best if the person you are interacting with has an open or willing attitude.

Just like words, nonverbal communication can be misinterpreted. People aren't very good at hiding their feelings and emotions leak out; but errors can be made when you attempt to decode these emotions. You should be careful because body language conveys important but unreliable clues about the intent of the communicator. For example, some believe that people with *shifty eyes* are probably lying. It is true that this non-verbal communication likely signals the presence of some kind of emotion but that emotion may or may not mean that someone is lying. Nervousness can, for example, manifest itself as shifty eyes and there are many reasons for nervousness.

Understanding and reading body language can also help you understand yourself. For example, you might catch yourself crossing your arms and realize that the body movement was triggered by a particular emotion. Awareness of your own emotions gives you valuable information to help manage your life.

SECTION 2 Other Makes and Models

While the body responds to the brain, it is also true that the brain responds to the body. Therefore, you should try not to have closed body language (e.g. cross your arms) unless you're cold or intend to put up a block. You will learn and experience more that the world has to offer if you are open and willing.

Paying attention to body language can aid in providing an understanding of what is really going on that words don't or can't say.

> The real success is when you can have more meaningful communications because of this attentiveness.

Interrupting

Compatibility issue: Interrupting others when they speak.

Resolution: Mindfulness, consideration and respect.

> *A good listener is not only popular everywhere, but after a while he gets to know something.*
>
> Wilson Mizner[33]

Interrupting is common communication misbehaviour. When you think you know the answer, have a quick solution or have something to say; you may interrupt when someone else is speaking. The problem is that when you interrupt you make the other person feel like his or her thoughts are unimportant. This is very unfulfilling for the other person. They may even feel that they, as a person, are unimportant to you. Therefore, interrupting is destructive behaviour, which you should avoid. Like everything, there are exceptions. For example, it would likely not be considered offensive if you interrupted to save someone from danger or embarrassment.

Unfortunately the bad habit of interruption is a difficult one to break. This is because it is the underlying behaviours that cause the interrupting that need to be dealt with.

First, interrupting begins in your mind. While listening, you begin to formulate your response. Often you haven't listened for very long before you decide the next thing that you want to say. You start to go over in your mind what you intend to say. You start to get more focused on your own thoughts and less focused on listening. Before you know it, you're talking.

Another underlying behaviour is that when you have something to say you feel that if you do not speak immediately, the idea will be gone and forever lost.

The behaviours of formulating a response while listening and feeling an urgency to speak, together, cause the interrupting behaviour. Once you decide your response, you put your energy towards remembering what you want to say, rather than being a good listener. The more that you think about what you want to say, the more urgent the delivery of the idea becomes.

You can stop the bad habit of interrupting, if you stop thinking so much about yourself and begin thinking about others. Everyone wants to be listened to and appreciated. Therefore, if you want better interactions and better relationships you must think more about other people's needs, rather than being absorbed with your own. Think about what the purpose of communication is all about.

Interrupting is a rude and disrespectful behaviour; making meaningful communication difficult or impossible. If you need incentive to stop the interrupting habit, consider how destructive it can be.

1. The "interrupting person" loses respect and regard from others.

2. Interrupting encourages both parties to speed up their

speech and their thinking. This causes nervousness and irritability.

3. Interrupting is the cause of many arguments because of the resentment that is caused on the part of the person who knows/thinks the other person doesn't listen to what they are saying.

4. An "interrupting person" can't really listen to what someone is saying when they are speaking for that person.

If you have the bad habit of interrupting others, remind yourself before a conversation begins to be patient and wait. Remind yourself to allow the other person to finish speaking before you take your turn. This new behaviour will improve the quality of conversations and relationships in your life because people will feel relaxed and appreciated. In addition, you'll feel relaxed and you'll enjoy conversations more.

Interrupting is a rude and disrespectful behaviour; making meaningful communication difficult or impossible.

Cause and Effect

Compatibility Issue: Undesirable treatment from others.

Resolution: Recognize that your own actions may be the cause. You can change how others treat you.

> *No one can make you feel inferior without your consent.*
>
> Eleanor Roosevelt[34]

Have you ever acted the clown and then were later upset when others didn't take you seriously? Have you ever acted aggressively in a situation and then felt the wrath of the aggression of others? Have you ever acted dumb or uninterested and then found that others didn't ask for your opinion? Can you see how the ways that others react to you may be dictated by your own actions?

Perhaps you don't like how someone treats you and you're thinking that in this particular case you've done nothing to cause the person to treat you as they do. Think again. If you receive mistreatment from someone, think on this - how have you contributed to encourage the behaviour? How have you reinforced or allowed that treatment? What did the person gain from their negative behaviour towards you? For example, if they were bossy did you defer to them and let them get their way? If they were a bully did you fulfil the role of their victim? If they unnecessarily criticized you, did you weaken yourself such that that they got the power they sought? If they blamed you for things that were not your fault, did you apologize? If they yelled and screamed, did you cower and make them feel big and strong?

If you don't like how people treat you, change it. You are responsible for your own life and this extends to how others treat you. It's not too late to change how others treat you. Insist on the best.

> If you don't like how people treat you, change it. You are responsible for your own life and this extends to how others treat you.

The Power Struggle

Compatibility Issue: After the "romance" phase of a relationship ends, many couples don't get past the next phase, the "power struggle", and the relationship ends.

Resolution: Awareness and effort.

> *Lots of people want to ride with you in the limo, but what you want is someone who will take the bus with you when the limo breaks down.*
>
> Oprah Winfrey[35]

All relationships go through phases. This is especially so for conjugal relationships. There are resources and professionals available to help couples understand the phases and offer suggestions to work through them.

There is a particularly difficult phase, the "power struggle", which couples go through. Unfortunately, many don't know that the conflicts associated with the "power struggle" are a normal component of a developing relationship. Instead they see it as the end of the relationship. Therefore, awareness of this phase is very important.

You accept that people are imperfect and yet you may have the expectation that your life partner should be perfect and that he or she should be your "ideal" man or woman. You want him or her to like the same things that you like and already know what you want before you ask. Until you spend a lot of time with someone and go through trials and tribulations with them, it's very difficult to know what they are really like. Often people will put a lot into a relationship and then just throw it all away during the power struggle. This is not to say that every relationship should be salvaged. For example, it may be best not to continue a relationship with someone who has fundamental, core values that conflict with your own. However, conflicts need to be put into perspective. Relationships require a lot of work and this is especially so during the power struggle. There is no perfect person. Instead of searching an entire lifetime with one failed relationship after another, would it not be better to find someone that you are attracted to; that is a good person with a good sense of humour and a value system that is compatible with your own, and make it work?

All relationships begin with a romantic phase. During this time, the needs of love and belonging are satisfied. Everything is wonderful and love is blind. The focus is on similarities and each does things to please the other. Differences are ignored. This romantic period may last two months or two years. Eventually one tires of being on their best behaviour and becomes the person they used to be. He or she tries to change the other person. There is friction and the power struggle begins.

During the power struggle, the needs of individuality and freedom want satisfying. Now, the focus is on differences and this is presumed undesirable. The war is on. Battles are fought over boundaries and what constitutes acceptable behaviours. The past is dragged up. When couples break up, it most often happens during this time.

The power struggle needn't be the end of the relationship or become the relationship. Couples can get past the power struggle. For those that do, there will be more phases with more hurdles, but none as difficult as the power struggle. Relationship goals beyond the power struggle include: accepting that differences are normal, being together out of choice and not need (as was such in the romantic phase), relating to each other as individuals and not trying to change each other, awareness of each others needs, mutual respect, a balance of togetherness and independence; and fun.

The power struggle is often unavoidable. Perhaps the power struggle is even necessary to achieve a long term loving relationship because it is this struggle that allows you to really know your partner and to let them know who you are.

Perhaps the power struggle is even necessary to achieve a long term loving relationship because it is this struggle that allows you to really know your partner and to let them know who you are.

Afterword

Other people provide many of the needs in your life and therefore they also provide many of the challenges in your life. The practical information given in this section can improve your interactions and relationships with other people. Best results will be achieved if you apply the information with awareness, sensitivity, understanding and patience.

Treat people as if they were what they ought to be, and you help them to become what they are capable of being.

Johann Wolfgang von Goethe[36]

SECTION - 3

PROCEDURES AND BONUS FEATURES TO MAXIMIZE PERFORMANCE

YOUR OWN DEVICES

PROCEDURES AND BONUS FEATURES TO MAXIMIZE PERFORMANCE

This section will explain some of the procedures and bonus features that will enhance your enjoyment of life. They are already included in your operating system – you need only utilize them.

PROCEDURES...
Section Contents

- Wonderment
- Fun
- Courage
- You'll Never Please Everyone
- The Meaning of Life
- Happiness

Wonderment

Procedure:	Wonderment.
Function:	Appreciate the world for all of the wondrous things it contains.
Maintenance issues:	Do not let disappointments or fears impair your ability to appreciate this wondrous world.

> *What is essential, I think, is to live life in wonder. All this magic that's around us, but we let it go by!*
>
> Leo Buscaglia[14]

The world is a wondrous place. It contains remarkable people, places, events and occurrences. It contains hopes, achievements, surprises and serendipity (the phenomenon of finding valuable or agreeable things not sought for). It also contains bad people, places and events; and hate, disappointments, loss and unfairness.

The challenge is to always see and appreciate that which is good in spite of that which is bad. As you make your choices in this wondrous world, do so with confidence. Explore and enjoy it in your very own way. You have much in common with others but you are also a unique individual. You have your very own strengths. What works for others may not necessarily work for you and vice versa. Just because someone appears to know all of the answers, it doesn't mean that they do. While others may appear confident they are often scared and insecure. Don't be intimidated.

> *I've lived a life that's full. I've travelled each and every highway. And more, much more than this, I did it my way.*
>
> Frank Sinatra[37]

Fun

Procedure:	Fun.
Function:	Fun is good for the mind and the body. And it's fun!
Maintenance issues:	Do not rank fun and play as a low priority. It is very important to your well being.

> *Without play—without the child that still lives in all of us—we will always be incomplete. And not only physically, but creatively, intellectually, and spiritually as well.*
>
> Dr. George Sheehan[38]

Endeavour to have fun. Fun is a very important part of your life. Yet, our work obsessed society often denies the importance of fun and relegates its importance far below that of work.

Fun is a state of mind. It's a time when you will feel most alive. Unfortunately, it's something you may take for granted and may forget to do. Also, many people believe that fun is unproductive, and therefore unimportant. This may make you feel guilty for having fun.

Your brain was evolved to have fun. Therefore, fun and play is instinctive and fundamental to human existence. Because of its usefulness in developing problem solving and adaptive abilities;

it is one of the evolutionary mechanisms that have enabled the human species to develop to its current state. Fun also relieves stress, builds self-esteem and adds balance to your life.

Courage

Procedure: Courage.

Function: Experience life's riches.

Maintenance issues: Keep system clear of irrational fears.

> *Our doubts are traitors and make us lose the good we oft might win by fearing to attempt.*
>
> William Shakespeare[39]

Richard Bach's[40] book *Illusions* begins with an insightful story about water creatures living along the bottom of a large river. The creatures cling to the rocks at the bottom of the river so that they're not swept away by the current. They do so from generation to generation because it is what their parents taught them to do. One day, one of the creatures decides that it is tired of clinging. Even though it can't see, the creature thinks that the river current knows where it is going. The creature decides to let go and let the current take it where it will. The other creatures laugh, taunt and predict that the current is such that it will throw the creature and smash it on the rocks to its death, which is far worse than boredom or anything else that the creature may be trying to escape. The creature doesn't listen to them. It "lets go". At first the current carries the creature such that it gets bumped and smashed on the rocks. But in time, as the creature continues to refuse to cling, the current lifts it off of the river bottom and the creature smoothly glides away with the current. As this creature moves with the current and passes other creatures along the way, the others see one like themselves flying. They think this creature possesses amazing powers. The "flying creature" calls to them "the river will set all of you free if only you dare to go."

The other creatures continue to cling to the rocks. When they look away, the "flying creature" is gone and they are left with the legend.

This story is a wonderful reminder of how limiting fears can be. Are you so different from the creatures clinging to the rocks at the bottom of the river?

Are you so different from the creatures clinging to the rocks at the bottom of the river?

You'll Never Please Everyone (Do What's Right For You)

Procedure: Be true to yourself.

Function: It is not necessary to please everyone or to be liked by everyone.

Maintenance Issues: Avoid the need for validation from others.

What other people think about me is not my business.

Michael J. Fox[41]

Aesop[42] was a legendary Greek teller of fables. The general consensus is that he was born around 620 B.C. as a slave. Legend has it that he was given his freedom as reward for his wit and his tales.

Aesop's Fables refers to a collection of fables credited to him. They have been passed down through the centuries at first by word of mouth and then in written form.

A favourite is the fable of *The Miller, His Son, and Their Ass*. Were you raised to always try to do the right thing? In this story what is the right thing? It all depends on how you look at it and from whose perspective. The following is from *Aesops Fables* as translated by George Fyler Townsend.

Excerpt:

"A Miller and his son were driving their Ass to a neighbouring fair to sell him. They had not gone far when they met with a troop of women collected round a well, talking and laughing. "Look there," cried one of them, "did you ever see such fellows, to be trudging along the road on foot when they might ride?' The old man hearing this, quickly made his son mount the Ass, and continued to walk along merrily by his side. Presently they came up to a group of old men in earnest debate. "There," said one of them, "it proves what I was a-saying. What respect is shown to old age in these days? Do you see that idle lad riding while his old father has to walk? Get down, you young scapegrace, and let the old man rest his weary limbs." Upon this the old man made his son dismount, and got up himself. In this manner they had not proceeded far when they met a company of women and children: "Why, you lazy old fellow," cried several tongues at once, "how can you ride upon the beast, while that poor little lad there can hardly keep pace by the side of you?' The good-natured Miller immediately took up his son behind him. They had now almost reached the town. "Pray, honest friend," said a citizen, "is that Ass your own?' "Yes," replied the old man. "O, one would not have thought so," said the other, "by the way you load him. Why, you two fellows are better able to carry the poor beast than he you." "Anything to please you," said the old man; "we can but try." So, alighting with his son, they tied the legs of the Ass together and with the help of a pole endeavoured to carry him on their shoulders over a bridge near the entrance to the town. This entertaining sight brought the people in crowds to laugh at it, till the Ass, not liking the noise nor the strange handling that he was subject to, broke the cords that bound him and, tumbling off the pole, fell into the river. Upon this, the old man, vexed and ashamed, made the best of his way home again, convinced that by endeavouring to please everybody he had pleased nobody, and lost his Ass in the bargain."

A wonderful tale! Need more be said?

I only write music for myself, I don't try and appeal to anyone else.

Bryan Adams[43]

I don't know the key to success, but the key to failure is trying to please everybody.

Bill Cosby[44]

The Meaning of Life

Procedure: The meaning or purpose of your life.

Function: It is your life. Choose a meaning or purpose that is your own.

Maintenance issues: It is not necessary to do something just because it is expected or just because it is not expected.

There is no meaning to life except the meaning man gives to his life by the unfolding of his powers.

Erich Fromm[45]

In W. Somerset Maugham's[46] classic novel, *Of Human Bondage*, the character searches for the meaning of life. After many unrewarding and ill conceived ideals, he fixates on a piece of Persian rug, offered by an old poet, as the answer to his quest for the meaning of life.

He sees that as *"...the weaver elaborated his pattern for no end but the pleasure of his aesthetic sense, so might a man live his life, or if one was forced to believe that his actions were outside his choosing, so might a man look at his life, that it made a pattern. ... he might make a design, regular, elaborate, complicated, or beautiful; ... There was one pattern, the most obvious, perfect, and beautiful, in which a man was born, grew to manhood, married, produced children, toiled for his bread, and died; but there were others, intricate and wonderful, in which happiness did not enter and in which success was not attempted; and in them might be discovered a more troubling grace."*

With this understanding of the meaning of life, the character imagines that he will weave a very exotic adventurous pattern. However, as circumstances unfold he is put into a position where he believes that he must marry to do the right thing and feels regret for the life that might have been. However, when the marriage is called off, he realizes that he had deceived himself. He had mistakenly thought that it was self-sacrifice that had caused him to think of marriage when it was really the desire for a wife and a home and love. What did he care for exotic places? This was here and now. He had spent his life following the ideals of other people and never the desires of his own heart. He had been swayed by what he thought he should do and never by what he truly wanted to do. What did he want out of life? *"He thought of his desire to make a design, intricate and beautiful, out of the myriad, meaningless facts of life: had he not seen also that the simplest pattern, that in which a man was born, worked, married, had children, and died, was likewise the most perfect? It might be that to surrender to happiness was to accept defeat, but it was a defeat better than many victories."*

Somerset Maugham's words speak volumes. It is your life. Choose your own pattern. You weave the threads of your life. You need not weave what others expect you to weave. Similarly, you need not weave anything new and exotic. You may choose to weave a pattern which is simple and been done by many before.

> It is your life. Choose your own pattern.

Happiness

Procedure: True happiness.

Function: Happiness is derived from within.

Maintenance issues: Do not use material goods or reliance on others as substitutes for true happiness.

> *I cannot always control what goes on outside, but I can always control what goes on inside.*
>
> Dr. Wayne W. Dyer[6]

What is happiness? Can money and good fortune bring you happiness? Are others responsible for your happiness?

Anicius Manlius Severinus Boethius ("Boethius")[47] who was born in Rome in about 475 A.D. provided some valuable insights about "true happiness".

Boethius was born into a privileged and fortunate life, was raised in the household of one of the richest and most respected aristocrats of the time and was well educated. He became one of the great intellects of his time and an eminent public figure. He had a loving family and the luxury of leisure time in which he pursued academic interests. One of his projects was to translate and interpret all the works of both Plato and Aristotle with the objective of showing the ways in which these two Greek philosophers agreed with each other. He never completed this particular project because the circumstances of his charmed life took a great turn when he was ... sentenced to death by torture.

During the course of events, that included Boethius defending a fellow Official from an accusation of treason, Boethius himself was charged with treason and sent to prison. During the prison sentence he was treated badly and tortured perhaps daily. While there, with his life in ruins and awaiting his death, Boethius turned to his knowledge and love of philosophy for comfort and wrote the book, *The Consolation of Philosophy*. After about a year's time, during which the work was completed, he was painfully executed (in about 524 A.D.).

While suffering in prison, rather than wallow in self-pity or rage in anger, Boethius used his experience to reflect upon, among other things, the nature of true happiness.

The story consists of a dialogue between a hopeless prisoner (Boethius), confused and dejected by his sudden bad fortune, sitting in his prison-cell awaiting execution, and a lady who personifies the subject of philosophy. Lady Philosophy consoles him but she does not console him with sympathy. Rather, she presents reasoned arguments that he has no good reason to complain because; true happiness can never be lost. Ultimate happiness is found in love and goodness.

The story uses Boethius' experience of a former good life compared to a current wretched life to show that fortune is a changeable illusion. It illustrates how due to this instability of fortune, it cannot provide real happiness. This point is taken even further when it is explained that because fortune is changeable, one must be concerned with losing what one has and this continuous fear does not allow one to be happy. This is so very true. You fear loss. You fear loss of relationships, loss of health, loss of material objects, loss of status and so on. When you feed this fear emotion, you do not fully enjoy what you have. Consider this: fear of loss is an illogical state of being because while you are not enjoying what you have, you may as well not have it.

Lady Philosophy tells Boethius that it is only a person's attitude that makes things appear wretched. To the person that has a calm mind and a positive attitude, things will not appear wretched. She goes on to scold because people look for their happiness externally, yet it lies within them. If one values nothing more highly than his or her own self and if they are in control of themselves; they will possess something of true value which fortune can never take away. Therefore, true happiness is not achieved by outward conditions because true happiness is found within.

> *Wherefore, then, O mortal men, seek ye that happiness without, which lies within yourselves?*
>
> Anicius Manlius Severinus Boethius[47], translated by *W. V. Cooper*

Afterword

The world is full of possibilities. So is your life. Be aware of this. Use the features described in this section to improve your life experience.

What lies behind you and what lies in front of you, pales in comparison to what lies inside of you.

Ralph Waldo Emerson[48]

Luck: when preparation and opportunity meet.

Pierre Elliott Trudeau[49]

Life is a great and wondrous mystery, and the only thing we know that we have for sure is what is right here and right now. Don't miss it.

Leo Buscaglia[14]

SECTION – 4
TROUBLESHOOTING

TROUBLESHOOTING

> *If the wind will not serve, take to the oars.*
>
> Latin Proverb

The world is not perfect. You're not perfect. Nor are your family, friends, colleagues, acquaintances or strangers. Things may not go according to plan or people may disappoint you. This section offers some suggestions for *troubleshooting* when things go wrong.

TROUBLESHOOTING
Section Contents

- Depression
- Disappointments
- Distortions
- Poor Me
- Negativity
- Anger and Forgiveness
- Grief, the Anger Stage
- Nightmares
- A Perfect Picture
- Unsolvable Problems

Depression

Problem: Bouts of depression.

Solution: Change your perspective. (Note: if frequent or prolonged, seek professional help.)

Trials give you strength, sorrows give understanding and wisdom.

Chuck T. Falcon[50]

[Note: There are people for which depression is a serious physical or mental health issue. These people need proper professional help. The ideas that that follow are for you if you (or someone you know) get into "a bit of a rut" from time to time.]

Almost everyone "feels low" once in a while. This is commonly referred to as "feeling depressed". Before discussing this, it must be clarified that this discussion is about the type of depression that is common to most people and consists of "having the blues" or "feeling down". It is <u>not</u> about "clinical depression" which is a state of sadness or melancholia that disrupts an individual's daily living and; it is <u>not</u> about chemical or hormonal imbalances that may trigger depression.

Many people feel that when they or someone they know is "feeling depressed", there is something broken that needs to be fixed and that it is in one's best interests to "snap out of it" as soon as possible. You may be one of these people and believe that the world would be a better place if no one ever got depressed. You can't change the fact that periodical depression exists for most people. However; you can change how you look at it.

When such depression occurs, there is often an external or internal disappointment that triggers it. If you are disappointed in others perhaps you need time to ponder and reflect. Behind your apathy or self-pity, a subconscious process is going on. The subconscious may be evaluating whether your expectations were too high, whether you failed to communicate clearly, whether you misinterpreted the experience or whether the other person is of an inferior nature. Accordingly, you must then decide whether to adjust your actions and/or perceptions. All of this will take a considerable amount of mind energy and it is not surprising that your mind might depress other emotions and senses in order to deal with the matter at hand. If you are disappointed in yourself or you experience a loss, you need time to ponder and reflect. While your conscious mind is feeling depressed, your subconscious mind may be healing and/or reinventing a new and improved version of yourself. Try visualizing a caterpillar in a cocoon changing and growing to become the butterfly - when the butterfly emerges, the depression ends. Another useful visualization is this - while hiking along the trail of life; sometimes you stop to rest in the shade and sometimes you step back to take a new path.

It is easier to accept occasional bouts of depression if you appreciate that it is a time to process, make decisions, heal or grow and that a depressed person may be better for it after it is over.

> Depression may be looked upon as periodic downtime for healing and inner workings for growth.

Disappointments

Problem: Disappointments.

Solutions: 1. Keep trying.
                           2. Look for the good or make the good.
                           3. Keep the mishap in perspective.
                           4. Give yourself a break.

Life has its disappointments. Do not allow disappointments to interfere with what you want out of life. How you react to disappointments dictates whether you will be a success or failure in your endeavours.

1. Keep Trying

<u>It's Not a Perfect World, Keep Trying</u>

Article after article, story after story, statistic after statistic: successful people do not generally succeed right away nor do they succeed all the time. Why then do many people, when they make a mistake or have bad fortune, give up? Are they lazy? Or, do they mistakenly think that because they made a mistake or failed, they are not talented or worthy?

Don't let your past mistakes or failures prevent your future successes.

> *I am not interested in the past. I am interested in the future, for that is where I expect to spend the rest of my life.*
>
> Charles Kettering[51]

> *I skate to where the puck is going to be, not where it's been.*
>
> Wayne Gretzky[52]

Common Sense, Keep Trying

> *Nothing in the world can take the place of persistence. Talent will not; nothing is more common than unsuccessful people with talent. Genius will not; unrewarded genius is almost a proverb. Education will not; the world is full of educated derelicts. Persistence and determination alone are omnipotent. The slogan "press on" has solved and always will solve the problems of the human race.*
>
> Calvin Coolidge[53]

It is human nature to feel afraid and overwhelmed. But look at all of the things you've already accomplished. Next time that you face failure, imagine what it was like when you learned to walk or talk. You likely struggled with it. Remember the mishaps when you learned to ride a bike and the feeling that you'd never get "the hang of it".

Failing is not a problem, but not having the resolve to try again is.

> *Whenever a negative thought concerning your personal power comes to mind, deliberately voice a positive thought to cancel it out.*
>
> Norman Vincent Peale[3]

2. Look for the Good or Make the Good

> *When life gives you lemons, make lemonade!*
>
> Author Unknown.

Sometimes bad things happen. They may happen due to bad circumstances, bad judgments or bad intentions. Often, it is difficult to not get upset or angry. Afterwards, what do you do? Harbour ill will? Find someone to say "I told you so" to? Put it out of your mind? None of these methods of dealing with the bad experience are in your or other's best interests. Why make the experience even more negative? Why waste the experience and effort without gaining something?

Something good can always come from every situation, no matter how bad or emotional the situation. Look for the lesson and if you can't find one keep looking and if necessary use the experience to break/change an old habit or start a new endeavour.

> *For every door that closes, another door opens.*
>
> Author Unknown.

3. Keep the Mishap in Perspective

Don't create a mountain out of a molehill. That is, don't overstate the calamity of the mishap. It's normal to make mistakes or have misfortunes.

4. Give Yourself a Break

> *Most of the shadows of this life are caused by standing in one's own sunshine.*
>
> Ralph Waldo Emerson[48]

Don't "beat yourself up". Remember your strengths and the good things in your life. Remember that things can always be worse. Focus on what you have and not what you have lost. Move forward. Don't be your own worst enemy. Be good to yourself.

> *Reflect upon your present blessings, of which every man has plenty; not on your past misfortunes of which all men have some.*
>
> Charles Dickens[54]

Distortions

Problem: Distortions in perception.

Solution: The test of scrutiny.

> *Courage is not the absence of fear, but rather the judgement that something else is more important than fear.*
>
> Ambrose Redmoon[55]

You receive and perceive information about the world. If you receive information that is compatible with your existing belief system it is generally accepted and absorbed. However, when information conflicts with your belief system it may be ignored or distorted.

You have hopes and you have fears. Often your fears (as part of your belief system) will cause you to view your hopes as far-fetched daydreams that will never come true. When you view your hopes in this way, you may have viewed them on a distorted basis. Consider this; more often than not it is your fears which are the distortions of reality and not your hopes.

If you really put your fears to the test of scrutiny, you will likely discover that most of your fears are irrational. If you really put your hopes and dreams to the test of scrutiny, you will likely discover that your hopes and dreams are not only rational but also feasible and that others in the same or worse circumstances have achieved as much or more.

> ...more often than not it is your fears which are the distortions of reality and not your hopes.

"Poor Me"

Problem: Victim attitude.

Solution: Take control and accept responsibility for your life. Refer to *Section 1 "How To" for "You"* for tools to gain control and stimulate a positive attitude.

> *Don't become a victim of yourself. Forget about the thief waiting in the alley; what about the thief in your mind?*
>
> Jim Rohn[56]

You'll go through a bad time once in a while. It may be a time where you undergo a significant loss or several major things go wrong at or around the same time. It can last days, weeks, months or even longer than a year, depending on the situation(s). This is natural. However, if you feel that you have had a bad time that has lasted a particularly long while, you may be suffering from a "poor me" or victim attitude.

People with this attitude say, "bad things always happen to me" and use this attitude to illicit sympathy, get special treatment or as an excuse to fail when they use feeble efforts in the first place. The need for sympathy from others may even be a disguised call for love.

"Poor me" people are not pleasant to be around. They're terrible as friends or customers. They're even worse as family members or work colleagues because you can't get away from them. They're negative. (See section on "Negativity" in subsequent section.) They complain and expect your sympathy. They see themselves as a victim - the world is out to get them, nothing good ever happens. Often, they're not reliable and when they let you down they won't accept responsibility because they believe it's not their fault (because they are suffering). They treat past events like a physical impairment and excuse to renege on commitments or not try very hard and therefore set themselves up to fail repeatedly. By not trying very hard to succeed and by being so miserable to be around, they have more losses and more hardships and push more people away. This naturally creates a cycle. The worse that they behave, the worse that things become and the "poor me" attitude is reinforced all over again.

You create your own life. You alone are responsible. You are responsible for your own happiness. Past events are not valid current excuses. Problems are unavoidable and pain is inevitable. However, suffering and playing the part of a victim is optional. You can choose to be strong. Misfortune is an opportunity to become stronger and better.

> *Birds sing after a storm; why shouldn't people feel as free to delight in whatever remains to them?*
>
> Rose F. Kennedy[57]

> *I would never have amounted to anything were it not for adversity. I was forced to come up the hard way.*
>
> J. C. Penney[58]

> *You may not realize it when it happens, but a kick in the teeth may be the best thing in the world for you.*
>
> Walt Disney[59]

> Past events are not valid current excuses.

Negativity

Problem: Negative attitudes are debilitating and contagious.

Solutions: Several. See points 1 to 15 below.

> *Don't be a cynic and disconsolate preacher. Don't bewail and moan. Omit the negative propositions. Challenge us with incessant affirmatives. Don't waste yourself in rejection, or bark against the bad, but chant the beauty of the good.*
>
> Ralph Waldo Emerson[48]

You protect yourself from catching colds and flu. You dress warmly and avoid people that are sneezing or blowing their nose. If you get sick you take a hot bath, drink plenty of fluids, rest and take medication to relieve the symptoms. If symptoms are bad enough; you may even see a doctor.

You may go to great efforts to avoid or get relief from a cold or flu and yet you may ignore an even more common ailment known as "negativity" (negative behaviour). Negativity is debilitating and highly contagious.

Recognition of negative behaviour is essential for prevention and cure. It's easy to identify if you know what to look for. A person experiencing negativity is seldom happy and is prone to find difficulties in situations. They tend to focus on the problems and pitfalls and not on solutions or opportunities. (They tend to focus on that which can't be done instead of that which can be done.) They may worry about things over which they have no control and may be quick to blame others. They are prone to exaggeration and cynicism.

Others may intentionally or unintentionally avoid you if you are habitually negative. Negative people tend to have less friends because no one wants to listen to complaints all of the time. The pessimistic, critical, doom and gloom attitude drives people away. Naturally this can impact careers and interpersonal relationships.

Negative people drain energy from themselves, (and because it's contagious) other people and even entire organizations. Therefore, negativity causes a loss of productivity.

Certain groups and relationships are particularly vulnerable for spreading and perpetuating negativity. Between family members, within households and among those with close connections, negativity is easily transmitted. At the work place, negativity is easily transmitted from management to employees and from employee to employee.

Children of parents that are negative thinkers are taught negative behaviour. Accordingly, it is often passed from one generation to the next. It may be that the pessimistic behaviour began with the intention to protect loved ones from life's disappointments. However, negative thinking does just the opposite because it does not teach loved ones the necessary skill of rebounding and trying again when it comes to life's disappointments.

To promote a positive attitude and avoid a negative attitude;

1. Ignore negative conversations or walk away. Avoid engaging in gossip or criticism about another person. When it's not possible or practical to avoid negative people, don't participate or absorb the energy.

2. Don't let the negative ways of someone else affect you regardless of who they are. Choose not to react to their negative words or actions. Ignore negative comments from someone that is always grouchy.

3. Have an awareness of the common types of distortions that negativity creates and know yourself well enough to recognize when you are becoming negative.

4. Form a support system with a friend or family member to help break the habit such that when one of you slips into negative thinking, you can remind and support each other.

5. Don't reward negative behaviour. Someone who constantly lives in negativity is getting some personal satisfaction from it. You can't change them but you can control your reaction to them and not provide any reinforcement for the behaviour.

6. Take a break after dealing with stressful situations.

7. Improve communications by taking time to understand and be understood.

8. Look for the positives in all aspects of your life. Look for the good in every situation. See that every situation could

always be worse.

9. Negativity may reveal a deeper issue such as fear. If so, the deeper issue needs addressing. In more serious situations, (e.g. paranoid, delusional or clinically depressed people) the help of medical professionals is needed.

10. "Vent" frustrations to a trusted friend or family member and then find a constructive solution or put the negative situation behind you.

11. Forgive yourself and others for mistakes.

12. Avoid or limit your interactions with pessimistic people.

13. Listen to other's concerns but don't let them just complain. Direct the conversation to a more positive way of thinking.

14. Recognize that people choose their attitude, whether it is positive or negative.

15. Spread humour and happiness. They are also contagious and counteract negativity.

All through this manual you've been shown how your attitude, whether it is positive or negative, influences your enjoyment of life. With a positive attitude you can enjoy life more, live longer and be healthier.

> *People deal too much with the negative, with what is wrong. Why not try and see positive things, to just touch those things and make them bloom?*
>
> Thich Nhat Hanh[60]

> *Our life is what our thoughts make it.*
>
> Marcus Aurelius Antonius[61]

Anger and Forgiveness

Problem: Inappropriate, misdirected or mismanaged anger is destructive.

Solution: Forgiveness, acceptance.

> *How many people we know who sour their lives, who ruin all that is sweet and beautiful by explosive tempers, who destroy their poise of character and make bad blood!*
>
> James Allen[1]

Your anger is nothing more than a reaction to or concealment of pain, frustration or fear. Often the person(s) or situation(s) at which you think you are angry, may not be the true source of your anger. It is common for anger to be misdirected. Sometimes the true source of your anger is a feeling of inadequacy or a feeling of unfulfilled expectations. If you can identify the underlying emotion that has triggered your anger and its true source, you have an opportunity for self-growth and improved relationships.

With awareness of the underlying emotion and the true source of the anger, you can pursue a course of action to resolve the conflict, forgive yourself, forgive others or forgive circumstances.

There is real power in such forgiveness and letting go. When you harbour anger, it harms you more than those (or that) to which it is directed. What can possibly be gained by losing control to those or that which has hurt you?

Hate, anger and resentment are destructive emotions. They impair your peace of mind and can impair your health. They rob you of happiness. They don't only adversely affect you; they adversely affect your relationships.

Anger is a natural human emotion. It is nature's way of empowering you to protect yourself. Feeling an anger emotion under appropriate circumstances is not a problem. Making anger a habit, mismanaging anger or not dealing with the true source of anger is a problem.

If someone has hurt you, be the better, stronger person and forgive the person who hurt you. Forgiveness is not about giving in to the other person; it's about regaining your own power - the power to be the master of your mind. You don't need to come to a mutual agreement with the other person. Just do it. You don't need an apology or an admission of guilt. Do it for you. Let the other person worry about his or her self.

If life has let you down, accept what has happened and move forward. This manual is full of suggestions to exert influence and control in your life.

How much more grievous are the consequences of anger than the causes of it.

Marcus Aurelius Antonius[61]

Grief, the Anger Stage

Problem: Feeling and expressing anger is often an unavoidable phase during the grieving and healing process. However, grieving anger can be misdirected and become counterproductive to the healing process.

Solutions: An awareness of the "anger stage" while healing.

Consider how much more you often suffer from your anger and grief, than from those very things for which you are angry and grieved.

Marcus Antonius (Mark Antony) [62]

It is important to understand that people that grieve go through stages. This is necessary for the loss to be assimilated and accepted. They experience a range of emotions that include shock, denial, anger and depression. The emotions are all part of a healing process. Different people will experience the emotions with different degrees of intensity and for different lengths of time.

Any type of loss can trigger a grieving process - loss of a loved one, loss of health, loss of a job, loss of a valued possession, etc.

There are many books and computer resources that deal with the grieving process. Also, there are trained professionals available to provide guidance. This section will be limited to the anger stage and with a view to creating awareness.

YOUR OWN DEVICES

For some the anger is felt at the beginning and for some it may not be felt until after a while. The anger may be targeted directly at the circumstances or it may be targeted at a spouse, a friend, a parent, a child or even a stranger. When anger is targeted at other than the circumstances which caused the loss, we say that the anger is misdirected. Failing to recognize and understand anger that is misdirected can cause conflicts that drive people apart and cause additional loss.

If you know why you are angry and at who or what the anger is really aimed, you can control the anger rather than allowing it to control you and avoid misdirecting your anger onto people who are important in your life. Examples of misdirected anger may include being unnecessarily critical, harsh or even cruel to family or friends. Misdirected anger can even be targeted at yourself through alcohol and drug abuse or otherwise allowing yourself to lapse into poor health. While expressing anger may be an important outlet of emotions it should not harm anyone, as this is counterproductive to the healing process.

Knowledge of the existence of misdirected anger is also helpful if you are the unfortunate target of the anger. You can be more tolerate, understanding and forgiving if you understand that the anger is not really about you.

> While expressing anger may be an important outlet of emotions it should not harm anyone, as this is counterproductive to the healing process.

SECTION 4 Troubleshooting

Nightmares

Problem: Fears and stresses of daily living manifest into nightmares.

Solution: Instead of waking up from the nightmare, use "lucid dreaming" to control and change the bad dream.

> *You must do the thing you think you cannot do.*
>
> Eleanor Roosevelt[34]

A nightmare is a dream that brings out feelings of fear, terror or distress. Nightmares often awaken the sleeper who is then able to recall the content of the dream. Most nightmares are a normal reaction to stress. It is thought that nightmares may help people deal with traumatic events.

[Note: Professional help should be sought if your nightmares are frequent or prevent you from getting sleep and performing your daily activities for a prolonged period.]

An effective tool to resolve nightmares and the underlying feelings of fear and vulnerability is something called lucid dreaming. Lucid dreaming is the state of dreaming while being aware that you are dreaming. Therefore, to have a lucid dream is as simple as to recognize that you are having a dream. This awareness presents you with the opportunity of controlling the dream. That means you can alter the dream and dictate what happens next. This is particularly useful if you are experiencing a nightmare.

If you've ever had a nightmare, realized you were dreaming and used the awareness to wake yourself up; you have already experienced a lucid dream even though you didn't attempt to take control of your dream.

When you know you are dreaming, you can remind yourself that nothing in your dream can cause you physical harm and you needn't run away from the source of your fear. (Actually, it is pointless to do so because the object of fear was conceived in your own mind; and as long as you continue to fear it, it remains with you.) The fear that you feel in a nightmare is completely real. It is the danger that you feel in a nightmare that is not real.

During the lucid dream state, you may be able to control and change the entire dream or you may only be able to control your own behaviour. Either way, the awareness provides you with the opportunity to confront and conquer your fears. Often, the nightmare will then transform into a peaceful dream.

For example: You are having a nightmare in which someone is stalking you and, in your dream mind, you have no doubt that this stalker will kill you. Of course you are terrified. Due to your intense fear, you realize that it isn't real. Instead of waking up when you come to this realization – you confront your would-be attacker verbally or physically (or anyway you like). You might say something like "You're just a big phoney. I'm not afraid of you." Your dream attacker might then change and shrink in stature and become rather comical looking with a funny grin as if to say, "You guessed it – I'm not a threat to you". You could then turn and walk away (in your dream) and never have the nightmare again. The benefits of such an accomplishment are twofold. First, you may never have the nightmare again and second, the experience of conquering the antagonist in the nightmare stays with you during your waking hours such that you'll feel stronger, less afraid and better able to cope with life situations.

There are uses of lucid dreaming other than dealing with nightmares. These include: gaining courage and confidence by controlling dreams, creative problem solving (experiment, invent, design and have conversations with experts) and the ability to experience unique adventures (such as flying or breathing under water). There are many books and Internet resources available on the subject of lucid dreaming. They offer suggestions for invoking, experimenting, controlling and prolonging the state.

…the experience of conquering the antagonist in the nightmare stays with you during your waking hours such that you'll feel stronger, less afraid and better able to cope with life situations.

A Perfect Picture

Problem: Can't manifest the ideal which would make you happy.

Solution: Be happy first, your ideal will follow.

> *One of the most tragic things I know about human nature is that all of us tend to put off living. We are all dreaming of some magical rose garden over the horizon - instead of enjoying the roses blooming outside our windows today.*
>
> Dale Carnegie[11]

Do you have perfect pictures in your head? If you do, there may be one for your home, your spouse or your vacation. Are you resolved to settle for nothing else because anything else would be incomplete or flawed? Are you putting off your happiness until the picture is complete? Have you spent a long time searching for and securing the "picture perfect" life?

Consider this, if you are waiting for just the right "snapshot" before you can be happy, you may never find happiness. This is because what appeals to you most about the picture you seek is that you imagine yourself to be happy in it. Because, you've put your happiness on "hold", when you view potential pictures, you reject them as unsatisfactory because the "happy" feeling is missing and you assume that the fault lies with the potential picture.

For example, some people desperately want to be in a relationship and yet they find something wrong with every prospective partner. Of course there is "something wrong" with everyone - they are human! A happy person seeking a relationship will focus on that which is right and will consider the person's faults with a view to whether the faults are things with which they can "live with". That is why those who search for a relationship for years; often find it when they quit looking. They quit looking because they resign themselves to be happy and content without the relationship. The happiness and contentment then helps them see things differently. It's the same thing with the dream home, dream job …

You have a free will and the choices that you make (or reject) are your own. Look at "pictures" with "happiness" and you may see something in them that you didn't see before.

Look at "pictures" with "happiness" and you may see something in them that you didn't see before.

Unsolvable Problems

Problem:	A particular problem presents itself and seems to defy solving.

Solutions:	Various – see below.

It's not that I'm so smart, it's just that I stay with problems longer.

Albert Einstein[4]

From time to time you may get stumped by a problem. Try as you will, there just doesn't seem to be a viable solution. The following offers suggestions to consider.

The first thing to do is to put the problem into perspective and determine if the problem is really a problem that requires your best efforts. How important is it that the problem be resolved? What is the worst that could happen if it is ignored? Is it really worth the effort? Do you have bigger problems that are being neglected? Put things into perspective. Don't ignore real problems by focusing on minor problems.

Also, don't focus on past problems or anticipate future problems. Present problems are difficult enough to deal with. Don't add to your misery by regretting the past or worrying about what might happen in the future. Live in real time.

If you consider your problem to be a real problem, the next thing to do is to determine if it is someone else's problem.

Feeling compassion for others and offering encouragement to others reveals the best of human qualities. However, you must accept that you are not responsible for how others think and feel - that is their responsibility. You may be responsible to them as a friend or family member, but you are not responsible for how they think and feel. If you get personally involved in other people's problems, you need to know that the person you are trying to help wants the help and is ready to solve the problem. In the absence of motivation to solve the problem, on the part of the person that has the problem, you, as a well-meaning problem solver, will experience countless frustrations. In such a case, it is vexatious to you to continue on the mission of solving someone else's problem. Accordingly, it is best to put your efforts towards more productive endeavours.

If there is still a problem that needs solving, determine if it is a problem with your perception. Some of life's difficulties are not necessarily problems. Difficulties can often be a problem of perception. The problem of perception can lie in your own personal filters or it can lie in your lack of knowledge or information. Therefore the solution to a problem may be to recognize that there is no external problem and the matter rests with you to clear the distortion.

Collect information about the problem. Problems are easier to solve once everything is known. Be logical. Why is it that solutions to the problems of others are easier to see? It is because when you remove emotion from a situation, you can think more clearly. You think more clearly when you are not subject to your personal filters and distortions.

Try looking at the problem in a different way. Ask - is this a problem or an opportunity?

If there is still a problem that needs solving, determine if the problem is just a symptom of the real problem. When focusing on solving a problem, make sure you are solving the right problem. It doesn't solve a problem by solving a symptom. Often attacking a symptom may make the problem worse. It is important to find the underlying problem.

Finally, if it's a real problem and it's important, don't give up. If you really want something - keep trying. Keep thinking, keep plotting, and keep scheming. Look for opportunities. Ask questions. Analyze each choice that life offers and ask "could this lead to…?". There is always an answer (although sometimes it may not necessarily be the answer that you thought that you were looking for); it just needs to be found. Worrying is unproductive. Honestly looking for an answer is productive. You are in control. Keep opening doors. Look inside of each door that you open and survey the potential. If it's not right for you, keep opening doors. If there is opportunity, go further.

A man will be imprisoned in a room with a door that's unlocked and opens inwards; as long as it does not occur to him to pull rather than push.

Ludwig Wittgenstein[63]

Afterword

Things will go wrong sometimes. This is a normal part of life. How you perceive and react to such situations will have a significant impact on your success and happiness. Having problems is not really a problem. Expecting otherwise or not having the resources to deal with problems; that is a problem.

For further information about some of life's challenges, see **Appendix 1, Frequently Asked Questions.**

People are always blaming their circumstances for what they are. I don't believe in circumstances. The people who get on in this world are the people who get up and look for the circumstances that they want, and if they can't find them, make them.

George Bernard Shaw[13]

A particular train of thought persisted in, be it good or bad, cannot fail to produce its results on the character and circumstances. A man cannot directly choose his circumstances, but he can choose his thoughts, and so indirectly, yet surely, shape his circumstances.

James Allen [1]

FINAL WORDS

FINAL WORDS

> *Fear grows in darkness; if you think there's a bogeyman around, turn on the light.*
>
> Dorothy Thompson[64]

There is a lot of straightforward and useful information in this manual. There are no games, tricks, tests, mantras or catch phrases ... just practical suggestions to help you enjoy life more. Some you already knew, some you knew but forgot, some you just hadn't thought about before and; some you will have received as new ideas or inspirations. Regardless of your level of comfort with your own devices - the important thing to know is: You already possess all of the devices you need to live an optimum life; you need only put them to effective use.

> *Obstacles can't stop you. Problems can't stop you. Most of all, other people can't stop you. Only you can stop you.*
>
> Jeffrey Gitomer[65]

APPENDIX I
FREQUENTLY ASKED QUESTIONS

FREQUENTLY ASKED QUESTIONS

To illustrate how this manual can apply to life circumstances and situations; "frequently asked questions", answers and manual references are provided below.

QUESTION 1 – I think that I "put off" some people. How can I get people to like me?

ANSWER 1 - In *Section 2, Enhance Compatibility and Performance with Other Makes and Models*, there are several segments that deal directly with matters that will influence how people react to you. In addition, *Section 4, Troubleshooting* contains relevant segments. Generally speaking, people will like you if they feel good when they interact with you and will avoid you if they do not.

There are some behaviours that can be very disagreeable to people and should be avoided (e.g. interrupting, insisting that you are a victim and a "doom and gloom" attitude.)

In particular, you should review **Words** and **Interrupting** in *Section 2, Enhance Compatibility and Performance with Other Makes and Models* and **Poor Me** and **Negativity** in *Section 4, Troubleshooting*.

QUESTION 2 - Why does everything bad always happen to me?

ANSWER 2 – The question suggests that you are thinking like a victim. Such an attitude can have significant adverse implications on the quality of your life. Review the segment titled **Poor Me** in *Section 4, Troubleshooting* and review all of **Section 1, "How To" for "You"** with a view to the things that you can do to change your outlook. Also, review the segments titled **Disappointments** and **Negativity** in *Section 4*.

If you can not gain control of the situation, you should seek the help of a professional Counsellor.

QUESTION 3 - I want a life partner. It seems crazy – people have been getting together since the beginning of time. Why can't I find someone?

ANSWER 3 – This is a problem for many people - you are not alone. There may be a number of reasons but the most likely reason is that you believe that you can not be completely happy unless you find your ideal life·partner. While you hold this current incomplete/unhappy attitude, two things happen. First, when you meet prospective partners, you "give off" this incomplete/unhappy energy. People are attracted to those that appear to be in control and are happy. Second, when you view prospective partners, you are considering their possibilities from the perspective of someone that is not content. Discontented people tend to look for the "wrong" instead of the "good". That means that you will likely focus on flaws and miss noticing a person's positive attributes.

You should review **A Perfect Picture** in *Section 4, Troubleshooting*.

Also, you'd better review the **Power Struggle** in *Section 2 ... Other Makes and Models* (to prepare yourself for when you do get into a relationship).

QUESTION 4 - Lately, I've been feeling a little down, is there something wrong with me?

ANSWER 4 – Experiencing bouts of mild depression once and a while is normal. However; frequent, prolonged or severe depression can have significant adverse implications on the quality of your life and should be treated by a professional (see your doctor for a referral).

Section 1, "How To" for "You" and *Section 3, Procedures and Bonus Features to Maximize Performance* contain various segments that will be helpful to overcome the "blues". Also, see the segment titled **Depression** in *Section 4, Troubleshooting*.

QUESTION 5 - I constantly worry. How can I stop?

ANSWER 5 – The segment on **Worry** in *Section 1, "How To" for "You"* contains some effective techniques to help keep the worry emotion in check. Also, you may consider reading Dale Carnegie's book *How to Stop Worrying and Start Living*.

QUESTION 6 - My friend always has problems but when I give her suggestions, she dismisses them. This really irritates me and recently I've been avoiding her calls. Why does she bother me with her problems if she's not going to follow my advice?

ANSWER 6 – There are a few things that may be going on. Some or all of them may apply to the situation with your friend.

You say that your friend "always" has problems. It could be that she is a negative person or has a "poor me" attitude. (See segments titled **Poor Me** and **Negativity** in *Section 4, Troubleshooting*.)

It is possible that your friend just wants to "vent" and is not looking for answers and that is why your advice goes unheeded. (See **Venting and Solving** in *Section 2 ... Other Makes and Models*.)

Another possibility is that your friend is unconsciously playing the game "Why don't you? – Yes, but" where she plays the part of the child and you play the part of the parent. (See the segment **"Why Don't You? – Yes, But"** in *Section 2 ... Other Makes and Models*.)

After you review the above and consider what may be going on with your friend, it is up to you to decide if you want to change the nature of the suggestions that you give to your friend or if it would be better for you to seek more rewarding friendships.

QUESTION 7 - I've always wanted to ____. But something always happens to ____. Is it just that I'm just not cut out to ____?

ANSWER 7 – This will be a long answer because there could be many reasons why you have been unable to attain your goal.

Your thoughts have a powerful impact on what you can achieve. Thinking that something always happens to frustrate your goal or that you're not cut out for what you want; operates to sabotage your goal because your thoughts, whether they are good or bad, go into your subconscious as ideas. Your subconscious looks for opportunities to manifest these ideas as events in the real world. Therefore, if you have positive thoughts, you are more likely to discover positive things. If you have failure thoughts, you are more likely to find failure. (See **Thoughts** in *Section 1, "How To" for "You"*.)

You experience this world and matters pertaining to your goal through your own perceptions. You react to and evaluate each event based on your very own belief system and attitudes. It may be that the way in which you see certain events, surrounding the attainment of your goal, is based on erroneous beliefs and negative attitudes. You should look for the weaknesses in your belief system and attitudes and attempt to view the situation in an undistorted way to better see the opportunities leading to your goal. (See **Filters** *Section 1, "How To" for "You"* and **Distortions** in *Section 4, Troubleshooting*.)

Depending on the nature of your goal, you may need to develop and improve certain skills. In order to become good at something, it is necessary to practice. (See **Neuroscience** in *Section 1, "How To" for "You"*.)

Successful people do not generally succeed right away nor do they succeed all the time. Therefore, when you make a mistake or have bad fortune, don't give up. Do not mistakenly think that because you have been thwarted that you should stop. Don't let your past mistakes or misfortunes prevent your future successes. (See **Disappointments** in *Section 4, Troubleshooting*.)

Perhaps you are approaching life with a negative attitude. Such an attitude makes one prone to focus on problems and pitfalls and not on solutions or opportunities. In addition, negative people can sometimes get into a "poor me" rut where they treat past events as an excuse for weak efforts that cause them to fail repeatedly. (See **Poor Me** and **Negativity** in *Section 4, Troubleshooting*.) Be positive. Be strong.

QUESTION 8 - Sometimes I get a feeling that something is going to happen and then it does. Am I psychic?

ANSWER 8 — It is more probable that your subconscious mind has responded to some stimulus that has not impacted your conscious mind. There is a considerable amount of information stored in your subconscious mind and that information in combination with the situation at hand, causes a "feeling". In the context of decision making, these feelings may provide clues to information that your conscious mind has overlooked. (See **Instincts** in *Section 1, "How To" for "You"*.)

QUESTION 9 - My father says that I should work in the family business. My mother says that I shouldn't work if I want to raise a family. My friend says I should go back to school to have a career. My husband says I should start my own business. I love them all. Who is right?

ANSWER 9 – You must look inwards for the answer. What do you think is right for you? You should do that which is compatible with your interests and your hopes and dreams.

If someone is disappointed about your choice - that is his or her problem, not yours. Don't choose a path for your life that is not your own choosing. Be true to yourself.

If you need help deciding what is right for you, read **Finding Answers** in *Section 1, "How To" for "You"* and read **Courage**, **The Meaning of Life** and **Happiness** in *Section 3, Procedures and Bonus Features to Maximize Performance*. If you need help dealing with the advice or complaints of others, read **You'll Never Please Everyone**, also in *Section 3*.

QUESTION 10 - Sometimes when I'm thinking about a problem, I find it helps if I do something else for awhile like going for a walk. I feel guilty doing this but it seems to really help. Why is that?

ANSWER 10 – Often there is an improvement in problem solving performance after temporarily putting a problem aside. This process is commonly referred to as incubation. Incubation is the experience of leaving a difficult problem for a period of time, then finding that the difficulty dissipates on returning to the problem or the solution suddenly become obvious while thinking about something else. Therefore, setting problems aside for a time and going for a walk can be an effective approach to solving a problem. (See **Finding Answers – 1. Incubation** in

Section 1, "How To" for "You".)

QUESTION 11 - If I could be financially secure, then I could be really happy - couldn't I?

ANSWER 11 – This question has been asked by many people in many ways. Often the question is phrased "can money buy you happiness?"

While it is true that a lack of money can be a disagreeable circumstance, some would argue that dealing with or resolving such a circumstance can add character to a person and meaning to their life; and therefore does not impede happiness.

To the extent that you believe that the circumstance of a lack of money impedes your happiness, you need to consider what you have done to create the circumstance. Your thoughts have an impact on what you can achieve. Thinking that you can't or won't have financial security may operate to sabotage your ability to be financially secure. Therefore, if you have thoughts that you expect to be financially secure, you are more likely to be financially secure. If you have thoughts that you will not be financially secure, your subconscious is likely to affect your behaviours and choices to make it so. (See **Thoughts** in *Section 1, "How To" for "You".*)

You experience this world through your own perceptions and you have the ability to choose how you perceive circumstances in your life. The existence of (or lack of) financial security is your interpretation of a situation and its impact on your happiness is your evaluation of a situation. (See **Filters** *Section 1, "How To" for*

"You" and **Distortions** in *Section 4, Troubleshooting*.) Therefore, a lack of financial security and its impact on happiness is very subjective. In other words, it is all in how you look at it.

If you have more money, that fortunate circumstance will not bring true happiness to you. Good fortunes can come and can go. True happiness is not achieved by outward conditions. True happiness is found within. (See **Happiness** in *Section 3, Procedures and Bonus Features to Maximize Performance*.)

QUESTION 12 - My husband won't talk to me when something is on his mind. He shuts me out. When I try to reach out to him and help, he gets mad and we have a big fight. If he loves me, he should trust and confide in me, right?

ANSWER 12 – Some people become introspective when they are upset, worried or concerned. This is discussed in the segment **Withdrawal** in *Section 2 ... Other Makes and Models*. You must understand that it is just his way of dealing with things and that it does not mean that he does not love you or does not want to trust and confide in you. Give him his space. You'll want to convey the message that you care and will respect his needs. In that way you provide him with understanding and support and he will talk to you about his problem, if he needs to, when he's ready.

QUESTION 13 - I hate where I work. I want to find a better job but I'm afraid. What if it doesn't turn out? Who will pay my bills?

ANSWER 13 – Challenge your fear. Is it rational? Why wouldn't a new job turn out? Don't let irrational fears cloud your judgement. (See **Distortions** in *Section 4, Troubleshooting*.)

See **Thoughts** in *Section 1, "How To" for "You"* for incentive to think positive thoughts, see **Courage** in *Section 3, Procedures and Bonus Features to Maximize Performance* to help find the courage to get free of your old job and see **Disappointments – 1. Keep Trying** in *Section 4, Troubleshooting* for inspiration to not give up.

QUESTION 14 - My friend lost his son in a tragic accident. I supported and helped him a lot when he was so sad that he couldn't even get out of bed. Recently, we had a big argument about something silly and unimportant. I feel betrayed. Why did he lash out at me?

ANSWER 14 – He likely lashed out at you because he is angry about his loss. Anger is a normal emotion to experience while grieving. Unfortunately, it is often directed towards someone close. Don't fuel his misdirected anger by participating in the conflict. His anger is likely not about you. If your friend continues to use you as the target of his anger, you may need to seek the advice of a Grief Counsellor if you choose to keep your grieving friend in your life.

See **Grief, the Anger Stage** in *Section 4, Troubleshooting*.

QUESTION 15 - My future plans are very ordinary. I just want to be a housewife and raise a family. Is this wrong? Should I aspire to bigger things?

ANSWER 15 – It is your life. You get to choose. (See **The Meaning of Life** in *Section 3, Procedures and Bonus Features to Maximize Performance.*)

Raising a family is a very important responsibility. Even though you intend to share the responsibility with someone else, you need to be financially and emotionally independent.

Before starting the family, it would be prudent to get an education and have job skills that you could utilize in the event that in the future you must financially support yourself or your family. Life can bring some unexpected twists and turns for which you may need the resources to deal with.

It is important to choose the right mate. However, you cannot control that your mate will always "be there" for you. In addition to preparing for the possibility of the unfortunate circumstance to have to "go it" without financial resources from your mate, you should also prepare for the possibility of the unfortunate circumstance to have to "go it" without emotional support from your mate. Preparation for this includes nurturing your own strength of character (numerous segments of this manual can be of assistance) and establishing friendships (and therefore a support system) with others. (See ***Section 2 ... Other Makes and Models.***)

QUESTION 16 - I work with a guy that no one likes and yet he walks around like he is superior to everyone. What's his problem?

ANSWER 16 – It is probably that he does not feel superior to everyone and is actually insecure. Often, people overcompensate for insecure feelings with arrogant behaviour. The man you describe probably feels afraid and alone and, like all of us, just wants to be loved and to belong. The more that these needs are not met, the stiffer he will appear because inside he is hurt and feels the need to act hard to survive. The stiff behaviour discourages others from getting close all the more (you mentioned that no one likes him). It's a vicious circle - the more he hurts, the more he pushes others away; and the more he pushes others away, the more he hurts. (See **Insecurity** in *Section 2 ... Other Makes and Models*.)

You can use this knowledge and understanding to better react to him and you may reap the rewards of getting to know the real person.

QUESTION 17 - Recently I made some big decisions in my life. I'm managing, but last night I had another bad dream. It's much like other bad dreams I've had. I'm being stalked and pursued by a dark force. I can't see it, but I know it's there. Fortunately, I realize that I'm dreaming and I'm able to wake myself up. It started just after I made the big decision - are the two related? How can I make the nightmares stop?

ANSWER 17 – Making a big decision can be a stressful time and after the decision is made, it is not unusual to have doubts or fears. It is likely that these emotions are being processed by your subconscious and have surfaced in your dreams. The bad dreams will likely go away on their own as you adjust to the changes in your life. However, there is something that may help immediately and perhaps more effectively than just letting time take care of the situation. It is lucid dreaming.

Lucid dreaming is an effective way to resolve nightmares and the underlying feelings of fear. It is the state of dreaming while being aware that you are dreaming. You mentioned that when you have the bad dream, you realize that you are dreaming and wake yourself up. The awareness that allows you to wake up is lucid dreaming. That means you can alter the bad dream and dictate what happens next, instead of waking up. Tell yourself that nothing in your dreams can cause you physical harm and you needn't run away from the source of your fear. With the knowledge that the experience is only a dream and no harm can come to you; you can confront your antagonist. The satisfaction that you will feel from conquering the experience in your nightmare will stay with you during waking hours and will help build confidence about the changes in your life. (See **Nightmares** in *Section 4, Troubleshooting*.)

QUESTION 18 - My brother in law says funny things about me as a joke but I don't find them funny and I feel hurt. If it's just a joke, why should it bother me?

ANSWER 18 – Humour is a form of communication. Like non-humourous forms of communication, it can be aggressive and mean-spirited. Just because an insult or criticism is hidden behind the veil of humour, it doesn't make it any less abusive. Bullies use humour to ridicule. (See **Humour** in *Section 2 ... Other Makes and Models*.)

You are hurt when your brother in law treats you this way – so try changing how he treats you.

The ways that others react to you are often dictated by your own actions. You may think that you've done nothing to cause him to treat you as he does. Think. Have you encouraged his behaviour? Have you reinforced or allowed his treatment of you? Does he gain from his jokes about you? Do you look weak so that he looks strong? Do you appear uncomfortable so that he appears witty and confident? It's not too late to change how he treats you. Insist on the best. (See **Cause and Effect** in *Section 2 ... Other Makes and Models*.)

If you're unable to change how he treats you, you can change how you view it. He likely behaves mean-spirited because he is angry, insecure or afraid. (See **Insecurity** in *Section 2 ... Other Makes and Models* and **Anger and Forgiveness** in *Section 4, Troubleshooting*.) If you understand the reasons why he is motivated to treat you as he does, you may feel less offended.

QUESTION 19 - My new colleague really pushes my buttons. Everyone else likes him; but he drives me crazy. Why can't they see what I see?

ANSWER 19 – It may be that the reason he bothers you is because you see in him what you don't like about yourself and have not consciously recognized. (See **Mirroring** in *Section 2 ... Other Makes and Models*.)

You have an opportunity to better understand and improve

yourself if there is a negative characteristic that you see in him which you also possess. Every character flaw that you identify in him is not necessarily a character flaw of your own. Rather, the particular character attribute that most bothers you is possibly a flaw or deficiency that you share (or in positive terms, an area for personal improvement).

QUESTION 20 – I applied for a promotion at work and I was turned down. I'm so embarrassed and disappointed. I won't go through that again. Really, how could I?

ANSWER 20 – Why do you think that you must be successful the first time you attempt something? If everyone had that attitude, humans likely would never have survived as a species.

Do not allow this event to interfere with what you want out of life. Such events do not reveal if you are a success or failure; but your reaction to such events does.

Read **Disappointments** in *Section 4, Troubleshooting* for suggestions on dealing with your disappointment in a constructive manner.

APPENDIX II

BIOS

BIOS

1. James Allen (1864 - 1912)

James Allen wrote about the power of thought. He was born in England. When the family business failed, his father left for America to make a living for the family but was robbed and murdered before he could send for his family. James left school to work to help support the family. He became successful and at 38, he retired. He and his wife moved to a small cottage to pursue a simple life of contemplation.

His books illustrate that the power of thought has immense capabilities. His most famous book is *As a Man Thinketh*.

2. Mother Teresa (1910 – 1997)

Mother Teresa was an Albanian born Indian Catholic nun. She founded the Missionaries of Charity. Her work among the poor of Calcutta made her world famous.

Her formal acknowledgements include the Templeton Prize, the Nobel Peace Prize, India's highest civilian award, the Bharat Ratna, the Pope John XXIII Peace Prize, the Presidential Medal of Freedom, honorary citizen of the United States and the first (and only person to date) to be featured on an Indian postage stamp while still alive.

3. Norman Vincent Peale (1898 – 1993)

Norman Vincent Peale was an American preacher and author of inspirational books. His most famous book is *The Power of Positive Thinking*. He was one of the first to teach the theory of positive thinking. He has inspired numerous other self-help book authors.

4. Albert Einstein (1879 – 1955)

Albert Einstein was a German born theoretical physicist. He is often regarded as the greatest scientist of the 20th century.

In 1921 he was awarded the Nobel Prize for Physics. His name has come to mean intelligence and genius.

5. Henry Ford (1863 – 1947)

Henry Ford was the founder of the Ford Motor Company. He changed industrial production in the United States and Europe and had great influence over the economy and society of the 20th century. He combined mass production, high wages and low cost (now referred to as Fordism).

He became one of the richest men in the world.

6. Dr. Wayne W. Dyer (1940 -)

Dr. Dyer is well known and respected in the field of self empowerment. He has written numerous bestselling books, including *Your Erroneous Zones, Meditations for Manifesting, Staying on the Path, Your Sacred Self, Everyday Wisdom, You'll See It When You Believe It* and *10 Secrets for Success and Inner Peace*. He has also created many audios, CDs, and videos; and has often appeared on television and radio programs. He is frequently featured on American public television (PBS).

He was born in Detroit, Michigan. His early life was spent living in foster homes and orphanages where he learned to be self reliant.

7. Dr. Phillip Calvin McGraw (Dr. Phil) (1950 -)

Dr. Phil is the host of the popular American psychology TV show, *Dr. Phil*. The show's format is that of an advice show. He is considered to have a behavioural approach to psychology where his style is that of encouraging the person to "get real" and to confront the issues at hand. He has also authored a number of books on subjects such as relationships and self actualization including weight loss.

8. Robertson Davies (1913 -1995)

Robertson Davies was a Canadian novelist, playwright, critic, journalist, and professor. He is one of Canada's best known and most popular authors.

9. Dalai Lama (Tenzin Gyatso) (1935 -)

The fourteenth and current Dalai Lama is often referred to as simply The Dalai Lama.

He was born to a farming family in Tibet. He was proclaimed the tulku (rebirth) of the thirteenth Dalai Lama at a very early age. When the Dalai Lama was a teenager, he became the head of the Tibetan government in their fight against the occupying forces of the People's Republic of China. After the collapse of Tibetan resistance movement in 1959, he fled to India. Since 1959 the Dalai Lama has been the leader of the Tibetan government in exile.

He is a charismatic figure and public speaker. His efforts in the cause of peace and a free Tibet have made him an international celebrity. He was the first Dalai Lama to travel to the West. In 1989 he was awarded the Nobel Peace Prize.

10. Dr. Richard Carlson (~1961 -)

Dr. Richard Carlson is an American author and motivational speaker. He is famous for writing the popular "Don't Sweat" series of books and audio products.

11. Dale Carnegie (1888 - 1955)

Dale Carnegie was an American author, lecturer and leader in the field of self improvement.

His books include *How to Win Friends and Influence People* which was first published in 1936 and remains popular today.

12. Dr. Joyce Brothers (Joyce Diane Bauer) (1928 -)

Dr. Brothers is a well known family psychologist and advice columnist. She was the host of her own television program, has published several best selling books and continues to appear on television and radio.

13. George Bernard Shaw (1856 – 1950)

George Bernard Shaw was an Irish playwright and critic.

He is the only person ever to have won both a Nobel Prize (for Literature in 1925) and an Academy Award (Best Screenplay for Pygmalion in 1938).

14. Leo Buscaglia (1924 – 1998)

Leo Buscaglia, Ph.D. was a renowned lecturer and professor at the University of Southern California (USC).

He was the author of several best selling inspirational books such as *Living, Loving and Learning* and *Born for Love*.

He influenced many with his insights into how people seek happiness and create loving relationships.

15. Joseph Campbell (1904 – 1987)

Joseph Campbell was an American professor, writer, and orator. He is best known for his work in the fields of comparative mythology and comparative religion. His writings include *The Hero with a Thousand Faces* and *The Masks of God*.

His studies and theories were made popular by a Public Broadcasting System (PBS) series of television interviews with Bill Moyers. The PBS interviews were also published as a book, which became a bestseller.

16. Huston Smith (1919 -)

Huston Smith is an American religious scholar. He is best known for his book *The World's Religions* (published in 1958 as *The Religions of Man*). His documentary films on Hinduism, Sufism, and Tibetan Buddhism have all won awards. In 1996 he was featured on Bill Moyers' five-part PBS special *The Wisdom of Faith with Huston Smith*.

17. Plato (427 – 347 BC)

Plato is a well known and widely read ancient Greek philosopher. He was a student of Socrates and the founder of the Academy in Athens where Aristotle studied.

18. George Burns (born Nathan Birnbaum) (1896 – 1996)

George Burns was an American comedian and actor. His career spanned vaudeville, film, radio, and television; with and without his equally legendary wife, Gracie Allen.

He performed for over three-quarters of a century. In his later years, he was better known than he was at any other time in his life and career. He died at the age of 100.

19. Voltaire (François-Marie Arouet) (1694 – 1778)

Voltaire was a French writer and philosopher. He was known for his sharp wit, philosophical writings, promotion of the rights of man and defence of civil liberties. He is considered one of the most influential figures of his time.

20. Graham Wallas (1858 – 1932)

Graham Wallas was an English political theorist and psychologist. He was a leading member of the Fabians who shaped Fabian socialism.

21. Margaret Atwood (1939 -)

Margaret Atwood is a well known Canadian novelist, poet, literary critic and one of the world's best selling authors.

Her books include *The Handmaid's Tale* (made into a movie) and *The Blind Assassin*.

22. William James (1842 - 1910)

William James was an influential American psychologist and philosopher. He is best known for his publication *Principles of Psychology*.

23. Charles Varlet Marquis de La Grange (1639 - 1692)

Charles Varlet Marquis de La Grange was a French actor.

24. Dr. Eric Berne (1910 – 1970)

Dr. Berne was a Canadian born, American psychiatrist best known as the creator of transactional analysis. He published technical and popular books on the subject. His best selling book was *Games People Play*.

25. Eric Hoffer (1902 – 1983)

Eric Hoffer was an American author. He won the Presidential Medal of Freedom in 1983. He came to fame with his first book, *The True Believer*, published in 1951.

26. Elmer G. Letterman (? - ?)

Elmer Lettermen was an extremely successful insurance salesman in New York City during the 1920's. He wrote books that include *The Sale Begins When the Customer Says No* and *The New Art of Selling*. He coined a slogan, "ABC," which stands for "Always Be Closing."

27. Elbert Hubbard (1856 – 1915)

Elbert Hubbard was an American philosopher and writer.

28. Malcolm Muggeridge (1903 – 1990)

Malcolm Muggeridge was a British journalist, author and media personality.

29. Oscar Wilde (1854 – 1900)

Oscar Wilde was an Anglo-Irish playwright, novelist, poet, short story writer and Freemason. He was one of the most successful playwrights of late Victorian

London. He was imprisoned after being convicted in a famous trial of "gross indecency" for homosexual acts.

30. Oliver Wendell Holmes Jr. (1841 – 1935)

Oliver Wendell Holmes Jr. was an American Supreme Court Justice and the son of the prominent writer and physician Oliver Wendell Holmes, Sr.

31. Carl W. Buehner (1898-1974)

Carl W. Buehner was a Mormon leader, businessman and author.

32. Ludwig Wittgenstein (1889 -1951)

Ludwig Wittgenstein was an influential Austrian philosopher who contributed several important works to modern philosophy.

33. Wilson Mizner (1876 - 1933)

Wilson Mizner was an American restaurant owner, playwright, screenwriter, boxing manager and con man.

34. (Anna) Eleanor Roosevelt (1884 – 1962)

Eleanor Roosevelt was an American political leader. She

was First Lady of the United States (1933 to 1945, Franklin D. Roosevelt).

Eleanor Roosevelt started out in life as a shy, awkward child. She grew into a woman with great sensitivity to the underprivileged. She became one of the most loved and respected women of her generation.

She was active in the formations of numerous institutions including the United Nations, the United Nations Association and Freedom House. She chaired the committee that drafted and approved the Universal Declaration of Human Rights.

35. Oprah Winfrey (1954 -)

Oprah Winfrey is an Emmy award winning talk show host and magazine publisher. She came from a humble background to become one of the most powerful and influential celebrities in the world. She uses her fame and wealth to positively influence the lives of people in need.

36. Johann Wolfgang von Goethe (1749 – 1832)

Johann Wolfgang von Goethe was an influencial German poet, novelist, dramatist and scientist. He wrote the two part dramatic poem *Faust*.

37. Frank Sinatra (1915 – 1998)

Frank Sinatra was a popular American singer and film actor.

38. Dr. George Sheehan (1918 -1993)

Dr. Sheehan was an American medical doctor, runner and writer.

39. William Shakespeare (1564 - 1616)

William Shakespeare was an English poet and playwright. He is considered by many to be the greatest writer in the English language. His works have been translated into every major living language and his plays are still continually performed all around the world. Many quotations and expressions from his plays have passed into everyday language.

40. Richard Bach (1936 -)

Richard Bach is an American writer. He has authored numerous books including *Jonathan Livingston Seagull* and *Illusions*.

41. Michael J. Fox (1961 -)

Michael J. Fox is a Canadian born actor. He was made famous by his roles in the *Back to the Future* trilogy and on the sitcom *Family Ties* (for which he won three Emmy awards).

He has written an autobiographical book, *Lucky Man*, about his experience with Parkinson's disease (with which he was diagnosed in 1991). Since then he has been a strong advocate of Parkinson's disease research - the Michael J. Fox Foundation was created to help advance this research.

42. Aesop (about 620 to 560 BC)

Aesop was known for his fables that contained morals and ethics. Legend has it that he was a slave in ancient Greece and due to his quick wit and fables, he was freed by his Master.

43. Bryan Adams (1959 -)

Bryan Adams is a Canadian singer, guitarist and songwriter.

44. Bill Cosby (1937 -)

Bill Cosby is an American actor, comedian, television producer and activist.

45. Erich Fromm (1900 – 1980)

Erich Fromm was a renowned German-American

psychologist and humanistic philosopher.

46. W. Somerset Maugham (1874 – 1965)

Somerset Maugham was an English playwright, novelist, and short story writer.

47. Anicius Manlius Severinus Boethius (about 475 to 524)

Boethius was a Christian philosopher of the 6th century. He was born in Rome to an important family and executed by King Theodoric the Great on suspicion of having conspired with the Byzantine Empire.

48. Ralph Waldo Emerson (1803 – 1882)

Ralph Waldo Emerson was an American author, poet, philosopher and orator.

49. Pierre Elliott Trudeau (1919 - 2000)

Pierre Trudeau was the 15th Prime Minister of Canada. He was considered a charismatic and flamboyant leader, particularly focused on human rights and civil liberties.

50. Chuck T. Falcon (? -)

Chuck Falcon is a counselling psychologist and author.

He is the author of *Family Desk Reference to Psychology*.

51. Charles Franklin Kettering (1876 – 1958)

Charles Kettering was born in Ohio, the United States of America. He was a farmer, school teacher, mechanic, engineer, scientist, inventor and social philosopher. He had poor eyesight and still managed to acquire an electrical engineering degree.

He believed that new ideas can be developed through cooperative team efforts and applied this belief to a broad range of interests. His inventions are numerous and impressive. He held more than 300 patents.

52. Wayne Gretzky (1961 -)

Wayne Gretzky is a former professional ice hockey player. He was born in Ontario, Canada. He is nicknamed "The Great One" being regarded by many as the greatest hockey player ever.

His many awards and achievements include that he is the only player to ever have his playing number, 99, officially retired across the entire National Hockey League.

53. (John) Calvin Coolidge, Jr. (1872 – 1933)

Calvin Coolidge was the 29th Vice President and the 30th President of the United States.

54. Charles Dickens (1812 – 1870)

Charles Dickens was an English novelist. He is widely considered to be a great writer of his time. He is frequently referred to by his last name only, even on first reference.

55. Ambrose Redmoon (born James Neil Hollingworth) (1933 – 1996)

Ambrose Redmoon was an American writer and rock music manager. He was considered a beatnik and a hippie. As a result of a car accident, he spent the last 3 decades of his life as a paraplegic in a wheelchair. He was not well known as a writer.

56. Jim Rohn (~1930 -)

Jim Rohn is an American author, motivational counsellor and motivational speaker.

57. Rose Fitzgerald Kennedy (1890 – 1995)

Rose Kennedy was the mother of President John F. Kennedy and Attorney General Robert Kennedy. She devoted her life to raising her nine children and was active in special education as well as in her sons' political campaigns. She died at the age of 104. She was well known for her philanthropic efforts.

58. James Cash (J.C.) Penney (1875 – 1971)

J. C. Penney was an American businessman and entrepreneur. In 1902, he founded the JC Penney stores..

59. Walt Disney (1901-1966)

Walt Disney was an American film maker who pioneered animated cartoons and created such characters as Mickey Mouse and Donald Duck. He founded Disneyland.

60. Thich Nhat Hanh (1926 -)

Thich Nhat Hanh is a Vietnamese Buddhist monk, peace activist, and author in Vietnamese and English. During the war in Vietnam, he worked for reconciliation between North and South Vietnam. His lifelong efforts to generate peace moved Martin Luther King, Jr. to nominate him for the Nobel Peace Prize in 1967.

61. Marcus Aurelius Antonius (121-180 AD)

Marcus Aurelius was the Roman Emperor from 161 to his death. He was also a philosopher and an author.

62. Marcus Antonius (Mark Antony) (83-30 B.C.)

Mark Antony was a Roman orator, politician, and soldier. He was the lover of the Egyptian queen Cleopatra.

63. Ludwig Wittgenstein (1889–1951)

Ludwig Wittgenstein was an Austrian philosopher who taught in England and had a significant influence on 20th century philosophy. His main works, *Tractatus Logico-Philosophicus* and *Philosophical Investigations* explore the relation of language to thought and knowledge.

64. Dorothy Thompson (1894–1961)

Dorothy Thompson was a prominent American journalist and political commentator. Her radio broadcasts and widely syndicated column *On the Record* informed Americans of the impending threat of Nazi Germany.

65. Jeffrey Gitomer (? -)

Jeffrey Gitomer gives advice on sales and customer service. He is an author of books such as *The Sales Bible* and *Customer Satisfaction is Worthless, Customer Loyalty is Priceless*.

66. Denise Lammi (1957 -) and David Wojtowicz (1959 -)

Denise Lammi and David Wojtowicz (sister and brother) are the authors of "Your Own Devices". They both hold the professional designation of Chartered Accountant. They have authored numerous courses for the professional development of accountants.

Their background and experience has well suited them to approach the matter of personal development in a useful and sensible manner.

Denise and David both currently live in Vancouver, Canada.

ISBN 1412095816